Lakȟótiya Wóglaka Po! - Speak Lakota!

Level 4 Textbook

Lakota Language Consortium

Pierre and Bloomington

i

Lakota Language Consortium is a nonprofit Lakota-led language revitalization organization.

Note: This is the student edition of the textbook. The next step in the sequence from the Lakȟótiya Wóglaka Po! - Speak Lakota! textbook series. It is designed to be used in conjunction with the Level 4 Audio CD (ISBN 978-0-9821107-7-5) and the Level 4 Flashcard set (ISBN 978-0-9821107-8-2) . The Teacher's Guide is printed separately. Please visit us at: www.lakhota.org for more information.

Lakota Language Consortium, Inc., Bloomington 47404
© 2012 by Lakota Language Consortium, Inc.
All rights reserved. Published 2012
Printed in China

17   16   15   14   13   12   1   2   3   4   5

ISBN: 0-9821107-6-6   (paper)
ISBN-13: 978-0-9821107-6-8   (paper)

Library of Congress Control Number: 2012931743

Authors: Jan Ullrich, Kimberlee Anne Campbell, Ben Black Bear, Elizabeth Allyn Woock
Illustrations: Laura Nikiel, Elizabeth Allyn Woock (pp. 10, 11, 26, 29, 44, 51, 70, 73)
Layout: Elizabeth Allyn Woock

Visit us at: **www.lakhota.org**

ACKNOWLEDGMENTS

This textbook was made possible through the contributions of over 50 language consultants and advisors from across the region.

We are thankful to: Dewey Bad Warrior, Ben Black Bear, Sandra Black Bear, Richard Black Elk, Gabe Black Moon, Florida Bull Bear-Jealous, Helene Circle Eagle, Marilyn Circle Eagle, Iris Eagle Chasing, Gladys Hawk, Paulette High Elk, Suela High Elk, Manny Iron Hawk, Philomine Lakota, Darlene Last Horse, Shirley Lefthand, Bernadine Little Thunder, Ken Little Thunder, Elisabeth Makes Him First, Helmina Makes Him First, Lyle Noisy Hawk Sr., Darlene Red Bear, Tom Red Bird, Mary Ann Red Cloud, Dainna Red Owl, Verola Spider, Edward Starr, Delores Taken Alive, Ray Takes War Bonnet, and Robert Two Crow.

There have been friends and supporters whose indirect help was critical to making this Textbook achieve publication: the LLC Board of Directors, the Standing Rock Sioux Tribe, the members of the Lakotadictionary.org Forum, and the many Lakota language activists around Lakota country.

The Level 4 Textbook was made possible through the generous financial contributions of: Administration for Native Americans, Native Language Preservation and Maintenance Category II - Native Language Project Implementation HHS-2008-ACF-ANA-NL-0016ANA Grant No: 90NL0429/2, the Tatanka Oyate Verein of Germany, the Moore Charitable Trust, the AMB Foundation of Phoenix, Jan Scherman of Sweden, the Sidney Stern Memorial Trust, the Onaway Trust, Sioux Chief Manufacturing Co., Inc., Lakota Herbs/ HPI Health Products, Inc., and an anonymous donor from Sioux Falls, SD. **Wóphila Tȟánka!**

Oglala Sioux Tribe

Sidney Stern Memorial Trust

Table of Contents

Table of Contents

Introduction

For Students

You've come a long way! There are lots of new words to learn in Lakota this year. Come with us! Let's have fun learning!

For Teachers

Your students can say a lot of sentences in Lakota now! But they need to go further. It is up to you to get the students to talk in Lakota as much as possible during class time. This is your opportunity to push them to expand their horizons and talk about different things. Use this book and the teachers' guide to prepare for each activity and to contextualize the language. You can make each lesson come alive.

For Independent Learners

You're ready to go to the next level! As you progress, sometimes you may feel frustrated. Every language learner feels this way sometimes. One of the most important things to remember is to make learning Lakota a part of your everyday life. Make a special time for yourself to learn something every day. Spending 15 minutes with Lakota daily will move you forward faster than cramming your effort into one day a week. You will see the results by the time you have finished the book.

For Parents and others who are supporting learners through the journey toward Lakota fluency

When your child or someone you care about is learning Lakota, they need your support! Show your interest in what they can say and write in Lakota. As a a parent or grandparent we need to also help them find time and space to study.

The Lakota language teacher needs your support too! It is important to be positive about the vocabulary words and sentences in the lessons. It is easy to be critical, but both students and teachers need all the support you can give them; even if they are teaching words you don't use every day. Students are sometimes introduced to words from other communities or to less common words. These variations make the language rich.

Here are some Lakota values that will help you in your quest to learn Lakota:

Wóohitike – Courage
Be courageous in the challenging quest of learning Lakota. Be brave enough to learn new words, sentence patterns and Lakota thinking. Your courage will be an example for other language students.

Wówaunšila – Compassion
Have compassion for others on this learning quest. Be compassionate with the errors of others and help them learn.

Wówačhaŋtognake – Generosity
Be generous in sharing whatever you have learned with others. Speak with them in Lakota every chance you get and where ever you can.

Wóksape – Wisdom
Gain wisdom by learning to love learning. Understand that no one knows everything about the language, and that we can all learn from each other. Your wisdom can compare various teaching materials and evaluate their quality.

Wówačhiŋtȟaŋka - Patience, Perseverance, Self-discipline
Patience and self-discipline help you persevere in learning. Never give up, strive in spite of obstacles and difficulties. In your daily schedule set aside at least two 15-20 minute slots for learning every day. Set a goal of how many words and sentences you are going to learn every week.

Wóyuonihaŋ – Respect
Show respect for the ancestral language by learning the correct pronunciation, spelling and sentence patterns. Value your language by respecting these standards; they maintain the authenticity and uniqueness of the language and culture. Show respect to anyone who learns Lakota regardless of who they are.

Wóuŋšiič'iye – Humility
Be humble about your knowledge and make your learning a life-changing spiritual quest. Don't brag about your achievements and don't use the language in destructive ways or for self-serving purposes.

Here is my picture!
(*paste or draw a picture of yourself*)

My name is _____
and this is my Lakota language textbook!

Here is some more about me (*answer as many questions as you can*):

Táku eníčiyapi he? _____

Nihúŋ táku ečíyapi he? _____

Tuktél yathí he? _____

Niyáte táku ečíyapi he? _____

Waníyetu nitóna he? _____

Nitȟúŋkašila táku ečíyapi he? _____

Táku waštéyalaka he? _____

Nikȟúŋši táku ečíyapi he? _____

Táku waȟtéyalašni he? _____

Oówa tukté waŋží waštéyalaka he? _____

Táku wamákȟaškaŋ luhá he? _____

Táku wóyute waštéyalaka he? _____

Táku olówaŋ waštéyalaka he? _____

Honíkšila naíŋš winíčhiŋčala he? _____

Taŋyáŋ owáyawa-ta yaglípi!

Show respect for your teacher and listen carefully to their instructions in class! Here are some things your teacher might say:

> Wówapi kiŋ natȟákapi.
> Wówapi kiŋ yuǧáŋpi .
> Núŋmnuŋm škáŋ po/pe.
> Wóečhuŋ # _____ .
> Blihélwičhaya yo/ye.
> Ótȟokahe.
> Tuwá wóyakiyaka he?
> Tákeya he?
> Niglúštaŋpi he?
> Akhé eyá yo/ye.
> Tuwá wínuŋǧa he?
> Yámni wíyuŋǧa yo/ye.
> Anáǧoptaŋ yaŋká po/pe.
> Ahítuŋwaŋ po/pe.
> Owá po/pe.
> Wówiyuŋǧe tȟokáheya ayúpta po/pe.

1 Watch your teacher while they say and mime the commands and copy them. Then say the command while you do it.

2 Have you got the hang of it? With a partner, pretend to be the teacher and give your partner these instructions. Then switch roles. Do you remember all of the actions when your partner is pretending to be the teacher?

Bob, Lisa, Matȟó, Summer, Mike, Tȟašína, James, and Kimi are back in school, too.
They're looking forward to learning Lakota with you this year!

1 Listen to Lisa and Bob talk about who they saw coming out of the bus. Number their friends in the order that they talk about them.

Mike ☐   Kimi ☐   Summer ☐

Tȟašína ☐   James ☐   Matȟó ☐

2 Fill in the blanks to continue the dialogue.

Bob: **Tȟašína** <u>waŋláka</u> **he?**

Lisa: **Háŋ,** <u>waŋbláke</u>.

Bob: **Mike waŋláka he?**

Lisa: **Hiyá,** _____ **šni.**

Bob: **Summer** _____ _____?

Lisa: _____, _____

Bob: **Matȟó** _____ _____?

Lisa: _____, _____

Bob: **Kimi** _____ _____?

Lisa: _____, _____

Bob: **James** _____ _____?

Lisa: _____, _____

3 Work in pairs. Play and then switch roles.

Student A: Choose one group from below. Don't tell your partner which group you chose.

Student B: Ask your partner who they see in the group they chose. Try to guess which group it is! Say the group number in Lakota.

4 The Memory Game

Work in teams of five. The teacher will place many items on a table. You have 10 seconds to look at the items before the teacher covers them. What things can your team remember? The team who remembers the most correctly wins!

Itówapi kiŋ waŋláka he?

Hiyá, waŋbláke šni.

5 🔊 Listen to Summer asking James about who he saw last summer. Cross out the friends that James didn't see.

Kimi

Mathó

Tȟašína

Mike

Bob

Lisa

Bonus Question: Who celebrates his or her birthday tomorrow?

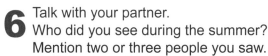

Híŋhaŋni kiŋ _____ tȟúŋpi tȟaáŋpetu kte!

6 Talk with your partner.
Who did you see during the summer? Mention two or three people you saw.

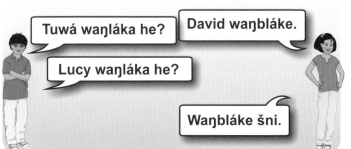

Tuwá waŋláka he?

David waŋbláke.

Lucy waŋláka he?

Waŋbláke šni.

7 🔊 Listen to Lisa talking to her grandfather about her birthday.

She says, **"Iná čhuwígnaka waŋ mak'ú."**
"Mom gave me a skirt."

Can you circle the part of the sentence means "me"?

Now, match the people with the gift they gave Lisa.

Iná

Até

Mike

Uŋčí

Mathó

Summer

Bob

Tȟašína

Kimi

8 Lisa is making a list of presents she got from her family and friends.

Can you finish her sentences?

1. Kimi <u>haŋpóšpula waŋ mak'ú.</u>
2. Até _____ eyá mak'ú.
3. Iná _____ _____ mak'ú.
4. Uŋčí _____ _____ _____.
5. Mathó _____ _____ _____.
6. Summer _____ ____ ___ _____.
7. Bob _____ _____ _____.
8. Tȟašína _____ _____ _____.
9. Mike _____ _____ _____.

9 The teacher will ask you questions about Lisa's birthday story. Answer with a full sentence.

How much of the story can YOU remember?

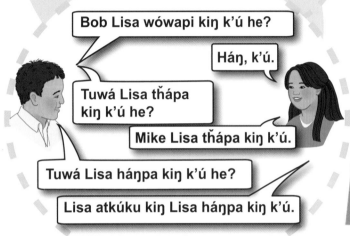

Bob Lisa wówapi kiŋ k'ú he?

Háŋ, k'ú.

Tuwá Lisa t̄ápa kiŋ k'ú he?

Mike Lisa t̄ápa kiŋ k'ú.

Tuwá Lisa háŋpa kiŋ k'ú he?

Lisa atkúku kiŋ Lisa háŋpa kiŋ k'ú.

10 Talk about one of your birthdays! Recall what people gave you and write a list like in the example below:

> Iná hunáhomnipi waŋ mak'ú.
> David wówapi waŋ mak'ú.

11 Look at your partner's sentences. Write what people gave to your partner like in the example below:

> David (my partner's name) wówapi waŋ k'ú.
>
> (Partner's name) húŋku kiŋ (partner's name) hunáhomnipi waŋ k'ú.
> _____
> _____ k'ú.
> _____
> _____.
> _____
> _____.

12 Listen again to Lisa talking with her Grandfather.

She says, **"Bob waŋmáyaŋg hí."**
"Bob came to see me."

Which part of the sentence means "me"? Circle it.

Listen and write who came and who didn't come.

> _____
> _____
> _____ waŋmáyaŋg hí.

> _____
> _____
> _____ waŋmáyaŋg hí šni.

13 Abléza po!

1. Which part of the word mak'ú means "me"? Circle it!

In the sentences below, circle the part that means "me." Is it always in the same place in the word?

Uŋčí wómak'u.

Kimi pȟóskil mayúze.

Summer íimáputȟake.

Bob waŋmáyaŋg hí.

Tȟašína mas'ámakipȟe.

2. Which sentences belongs to each picture? Write in one sentence from the Abléza po! next to the correct picture.

14 Write in the missing "ma." Think carefully about where it goes.

k'ú	_mak'ú_
wók'u	_____
waŋyáŋg hí	_____
pȟóskil yúze	_____
mas'ákipȟe	_____
íipútȟake	_____

15 Lisa is really excited to tell James all about the gifts that she got for her birthday. Read through the texts they sent each other and answer the questions below.

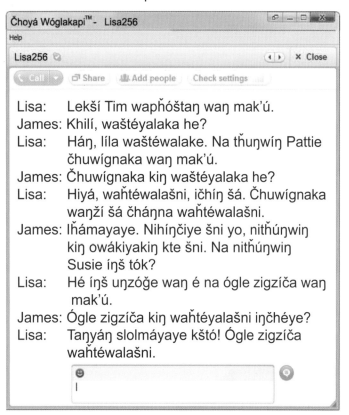

Čhoyá Wóglakapi™ - Lisa256

Help

Lisa256 ◁ ▷ ✕ Close

Call ▾ ⊡ Share ⬚ Add people Check settings

Lisa: Lekší Tim waphóštaŋ waŋ mak'ú.
James: Khilí, waštéyalaka he?
Lisa: Háŋ, líla waštéwalake. Na tȟuŋwíŋ Pattie čhuwígnaka waŋ mak'ú.
James: Čhuwígnaka kiŋ waštéyalaka he?
Lisa: Hiyá, waȟtéwalašni, ičhíŋ šá. Čhuwígnaka waŋží šá čháŋna waȟtéwalašni.
James: Iȟámayaye. Nihíŋčiye šni yo, nitȟúŋwiŋ kiŋ owákiyakiŋ kte šni. Na nitȟúŋwiŋ Susie íŋš tók?
Lisa: Hé íŋš uŋzóǧe waŋ é na ógle zigzíča waŋ mak'ú.
James: Ógle zigzíča kiŋ waȟtéyalašni iŋčhéye?
Lisa: Taŋyáŋ slolmáyaye kštó! Ógle zigzíča waȟtéwalašni.

☺
|

a Which items does Lisa like? Put a check next to those items.

waphóštaŋ **čhuwígnaka** **ógle zigzíča**

b Which items does Lisa dislike? Put an "x" next to those items.

16 Abléza po!

How do we talk about liking and disliking things? Draw a smiley face next to the sentence that talks about liking something. Draw a frowny face next to the sentence that talks about disliking something.

◯ **Lisa waphóštaŋ kiŋ waštélake.**

◯ **Lisa čhuwígnake kiŋ waȟtélašni.**

17 All the children are talking about gifts they were given for their birthdays. Do they like them or not? On a piece of scratch paper, write sentences about what each child below likes and doesn't like, just as the example.

Iyéčhiŋkyaŋke kiŋ waštéwalake.

Kiŋyékhiyapi kiŋ waȟtéwalašni.

Haŋpóšpula kiŋ waštéwalake.

Omás'apȟela kiŋ waštéwalake.

Matȟóla kiŋ waȟtéwalašni.

Bob iyéčhiŋkyaŋke kiŋ waštélake.

18 Now, stand in a circle with your classmates. Your teacher will give you a role play card with a gift on it. Give the gift to someone else in the circle. Then, you will talk about what you got, like the model.

Susie tȟápa waŋ mak'ú.
Tȟápa kiŋ lé waštéwalake.

Jamie wíčazo waŋ mak'ú.
Wíčazo kiŋ lé waȟtéwalašni.

19 Now, write about what just happened in your class! Talk about 3 or 4 of your classmates. Who gave what to whom? Did they like it or not? Write 6-8 sentences on scrap paper.

20 The children are telling us about what someone did to them yesterday.

a Your teacher will say these sentences. Respond with the number of the correct sentence.

b Now, your teacher will say a sentence. Repeat it and mime the activity.

Bob mas'ámakipȟe.

Hokšíla kiŋ hé aímaȟat'e.

Mike amáčhaŋzeke.

Kimi themáȟila.

Hokšíla kiŋ hé amápȟe.

Waúŋspewičhakhiye kiŋ napé mayúze.

Misúŋkala yuš'íŋyemaye.

Kimi pȟóskil mayúze.

Lisa wómak'u.

Hokšíla kiŋ hé namáȟtake.

č Now your teacher will say a number and you will say the sentence!

21

Let's play charades! Make groups, with three or four students in each group. One student chooses a picture from Exercise 20 to mime. The other teammates try to identify which picture it is. Nod if your teammates are correct.

22 Read the statement and rewrite it as a report (**reported speech**) like the example.

a Lisa heyé: "Kimi themáȟila," eyé.

Kimi Lisa theȟíla

b Tȟašína heyé: "Kimi pȟóskil mayúze," eyé.

_____

č Matȟó heyé: "Mike amáčhaŋzeke," eyé.

_____

e Mike heyé: "Bob mas'ámakipȟe," eyé.

_____

g James heyé: "Hokšíla kiŋ hé aímaȟat'e," eyé.

_____

23 Read the statement and fill in the speech bubble for each character.

Robert Mike napé yúze.

Robert napé mayúze.

Mike

Summer Lisa wók'u.

Lisa

Tȟašína Summer apȟé.

Summer

Šúŋkawakȟáŋ kiŋ Matȟó naȟtáke.

Mat□ó

24 Write a short story about what happened at your last birthday. Who came? What did they give you?

Barbie waŋmáyaŋg hí.
Iná pȟóskil mayúze.
Tom wówapi waŋ mak'ú.

_____
_____
_____

25

Look at the first pair of sentences. How are they different?
Write in the missing ending "**-pi**" to make these sentences plural.
Which of the verbs below are ablaut verbs? Circle them. How can you tell?

Aímaȟat'e.

Aímaȟat'api.

Amáčhaŋzeke.

Amáčhaŋzeka___.

Yuš'íŋyemaye.

Yuš'íŋyemayaŋ___.

Amáyuta.

Amáyuta___.

26

Match the sentences with the correct pictures.

Amáyutapi.

Aímaȟat'api.

Amáčhaŋzeke.

Yuš'íŋyemayaŋpi.

Aímaȟat'e.

Yuš'íŋyemaye.

27

What is the plural ending?
How many people are doing the activity,
one or more? Listen and circle.

1

2

3

4

28

> Bob and Lisa want their Lakota pronunciation to sound as beautiful as their grandparents', so they are practicing Lakota vowels.
>
> Practice with them!

> Do you remember which letters are vowels?
>
> **They are A, E, I, O and U!**

A Listen to your teacher or the recording and try to copy the sound.

Try to repeat the **A** with a rhythm!

A! A! A! A! A! A! A! A! A! A!

Try saying **A** with these words:
1) há, na, ká, lá, šá, wá, yá
2) hála, sápa, waná, kaná, čháŋna, škáta, čhápa

Now, try this sentence! Can you say **A** perfectly?
Hála waŋ lúta čha škáta čha ablúta.

E Listen to your teacher or the recording and try to copy the sound.

Try to repeat the **E** with a rhythm!

E! E! E! E! E! E! E! E! E! E!

Try saying **E** with these words:
1) hé, lé, ȟé, we, ye, é
2) napé, até, bébela, khéya, hená, héčha, hehehé

Now, try this sentence! Can you say **E** perfectly?
Khéya waŋ šápe kiŋ lé pȟeží háŋska yúte.

I

Listen to your teacher or the recording and try to copy the sound.

Try to repeat the **I** with a rhythm!

Try saying **I** with these words:
1) sí, zí, hí, ní, ǧí, khí, phí
2) sihá, iná, zičá, pȟeží, uŋčí, thípi, thezí, máni

Now, try this sentence! Can you say **I** perfectly?
Iná thípi waŋ zí kiŋ thimá í.

O

Listen to your teacher or the recording and try to copy the sound.

Try to repeat the **O** with a rhythm!

Try saying **O** with these words:
1) ó, po, bló, wo, yo, žó, čhó, hó, hwo, tȟó, kȟó
2) oówa, óta, matȟó, ógle, tópa, tóna, ȟóta, istó

Now, try this sentence! Can you say **O** perfectly?
Matȟó waŋ ištá tȟotȟó kiŋ istó popó.

U

Listen to your teacher or the recording and try to copy the sound.

Try to repeat the **U** with a rhythm!

Try saying **U** with these words:
1) ú, sú, hú, kú, bú, čhú, ǧú,
2) úta, makhú, ikhú, pȟasú, púza, khukhúše

Now, try this sentence! Can you say **U** perfectly?
Khukhúše waŋ úta waŋ púza čha ayúta.

29 Fill in the missing words on the horse picture.

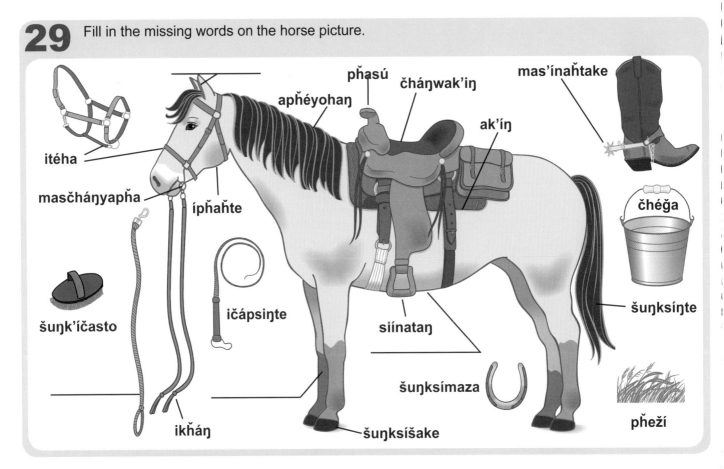

pȟasú

čháŋwak'iŋ

mas'ínaȟtake

apȟéyohaŋ

ak'íŋ

itéha

masčháŋyapȟa

ípȟaȟte

čhéǧa

šuŋk'íčasto

ičápsiŋte

šuŋksíŋte

siínataŋ

šuŋksímaza

ikȟáŋ

šuŋksíšake

pȟeží

30 Look at the picture of the corral. Does anyone in your family do these activities, too? Write down three examples on a piece of scrap paper, like the example below. Then, share them with your partner.

Até šuŋk'ákaŋyaŋke.

kaúŋspe

čháŋwak'iŋ iyákaškA

šuŋk'ákaŋyaŋkA

čháŋwak'iŋ khí

kastó

wók'u

31 Match the horses with the names of their colors.

híŋȟota

híŋša

híŋzi

šuŋgsápA

šuŋgská

šuŋgléška

hiŋíkčeka

32 🔊 Bob is talking about his uncle's ranch and what they do there. Listen to what he says, and draw lines to match the person with the horse, the things they do, and the items they use.

33 Your partner will choose one of the barns below. Can you guess which one? Ask him or her questions to figure out which barn he/she is thinking of, like the example.

Šuŋgsápa waŋží waŋláka he?

_____ waŋží waŋláka he?

Eháŋuŋ! Ťȟózi kiŋ hé é!

Háŋ, šuŋgsápa waŋ waŋbláke. /
Hiyá, šuŋgsápa waŋžíni waŋbláke šni.

Háŋ, _____ waŋ waŋbláke. /
Hiyá, _____ waŋžíni waŋbláke šni.

34 Bob is reading a story that his great-grandfather wrote about his youth. First, use your glossary to find the meaning of the four underlined words. Then, skim through the text and pictures and, with a partner, think of a title for the story. Write the title in the space below.

_____

1 Eháŋni kȟomáškalaka k'uŋ héhaŋ <u>zuyá yápi</u> waŋ él ówapȟa.

2 <u>Šuŋmánuŋ</u> uŋyáŋpi.

3 Šúŋkawakȟáŋ waŋ kȟaŋháŋskeya kašká nážiŋ čha waŋbláke. Ho čha mawánuŋ kta čha ikhíyela waí.

4 Šúŋka waŋ nam**á**ȟ'uŋ na ma**p**ȟápȟa.

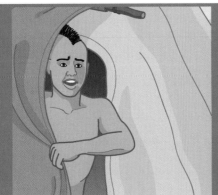

5 Yuŋkȟáŋ <u>tȟóka</u> waŋ tȟaŋkál hiyú na waŋ**m**áyaŋke.

6 M**a**khúte, éyaš wo**m**ášna.

14

7 Yuŋkȟáŋ šúŋkawakȟáŋ kiŋ **m**apáȟpe.

8 Toháŋyaŋ owákihika waíŋmnaŋke, éyaš tȟóka kiŋ **m**akȟúwa.

9 **M**akígleğiŋ na **m**akȟíza yuŋkȟáŋ <u>ihúŋničatȟa</u> waŋ uŋ a**m**ápȟe.

10 Kȟoláwaya waŋ hihúŋni na ó**m**akiye ló.

11 Yuŋkȟáŋ naúŋpȟapi na niúŋkič'iyapi.

35 Match the person or animal with the things that they did in the story.

tȟóka

naȟ'úŋ
waŋyáŋkA
pȟapȟá
wošná
paȟpÁ
khuwá
kigléǧA
khízA
apȟÁ
ókiyA
khuté

šúŋka

šúŋkawakȟáŋ

kȟoláya waŋ

37 Write the sentences from activity 34 as if you were telling the story yourself.

First, look at the example. What do you need to add to the verb?

Šúŋka waŋ mapȟápȟa.

36 Who did what to the boy in the story? Using the information from the story, fill in the missing part of the sentence, like in the example.

Šúŋka waŋ kȟoškálaka ___kiŋ naȟ'úŋ___ .

_____waŋ kȟoškálaka kiŋ waŋyáŋke.

Šúŋka waŋ kȟoškálaka kiŋ _____ .

Tȟóka kiŋ kȟoškálaka kiŋ _____ .

_____ kȟoškálaka kiŋ wošná.

Šúŋkawakȟaŋ kiŋ kȟoškálaka kiŋ _____ .

_____ kȟoškálaka kiŋ khuwá.

_____ kȟoškálaka kiŋ kigléǧe.

_____ kȟoškálaka kiŋ khíze.

_____ kȟoškálaka kiŋ ihúŋničatȟa uŋ apȟé.

Kȟoláya waŋ kȟoškálaka kiŋ _____ .

Review Quiz

1 Who got what from whom on their birthdays? Can you answer these questions according to the pictures?

a Táku čha Lisa Bob k'ú he?

b Tuwá Summer ikȟáŋ etáŋ k'ú he?

č Táku čha James Mike k'ú he?

e Tuwá Mike ičápsiŋte waŋží k'ú he?

g Táku čha Matȟó Lisa k'ú he?

ǧ Tuwá Matȟó itéha waŋží k'ú he?

2 What did you get for your last birthday? Pick out 3 or 4 things that you know how to say in Lakȟóta. Then write sentences about who gave you those things, like the model:

Até wówapi waŋ mak'ú.

3 What happened to you today in school? Pretend each time that the picture is happening to you! Can you write sentences about your day, like the example here?

Wičháša kiŋ hé napé mayúze.

Hokšila kiŋ hé _____

Hokšila kiŋ hé _____

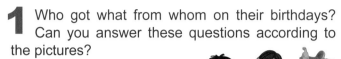
_____

_____

_____

_____

4 Here is a story of Bob's day with the horses out at his uncle's ranch. But parts of the story are out of order! Can you figure out the correct order, and finish numbering the sentences?

1 Lekšítku kiŋ pteyúha othí waŋ yuhá.

2 Šúŋkawakȟáŋ óta wičháyuha.

3 Bob šúŋkawakȟáŋ kiŋ hená líla waštéwičhalake.

____ Pteyúha othí kiŋ él, Bob šuŋgléška waŋ waŋyáŋke.

____ Šúŋka waŋ Bob é na šúŋkawakȟáŋ tȟáwa kiŋ wičhápȟapȟa.

____ Tȟokáheya Bob šuŋgléška k'uŋ hé kastó.

____ Yuŋkȟáŋ šúŋkawakȟáŋ kiŋ hé Bob paȟpé.

____ Bob pteyúha othí kiŋ ektá máni hí.

____ Bob šuŋk'ákaŋyaŋke!

____ Heháŋl čháŋwak'iŋ waŋ iyákaške.

____ Šúŋka kiŋ hé šúŋkawakȟáŋ kiŋ hé yuš'íŋyeye.

____ Ehákeȟčiŋ wók'u.

____ Šúŋkawakȟáŋ k'uŋ waŋyáŋka čhaŋkhé čháŋwak'iŋ khí.

1 🔊 Matȟó is getting ready for a fishing trip. Listen to James talking to Matȟó about what Matho's relatives gave him for the trip. Number the items in the order that he mentions them.

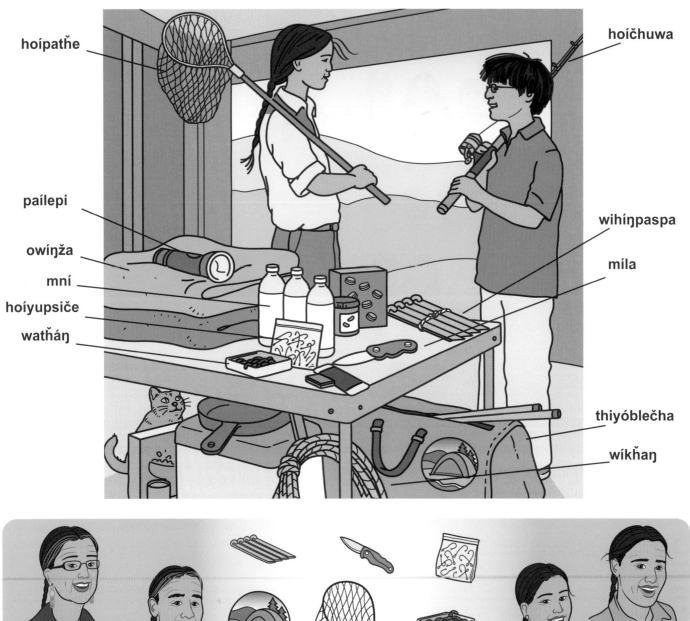

hoípatȟe

hoíčhuwa

paílepi

owíŋža

mní

hoíyupsiče

watȟáŋ

wihíŋpaspa

míla

thiyóbleča

wíkȟaŋ

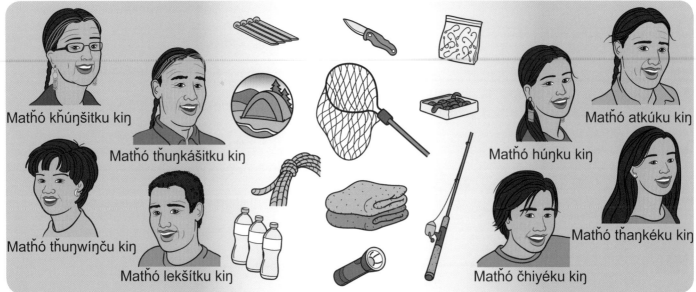

Matȟó kȟúŋšitku kiŋ

Matȟó tȟuŋkášitku kiŋ

Matȟó tȟuŋwíŋcu kiŋ

Matȟó lekšítku kiŋ

Matȟó húŋku kiŋ

Matȟó atkúku kiŋ

Matȟó tȟaŋkéku kiŋ

Matȟó čhiyéku kiŋ

2 Now listen again and draw lines to match the people with the items that they gave to Matȟó. Some people gave more than one item.

3 Bob is also going on a fishing trip!
Read the dialogue and answer the questions below:

Mike: Niyáte kiŋ táku nič'ú he?
Bob: Até thiyóblečha kiŋ lé mak'ú.

a How does Bob say "*He gave me*"?
Write it here _____

b How does Mike say "*He gave you*"?
Write it here _____

č How does the spelling of the verb **k'ú** change when you put **ni-** (*you*) in front of it? What is different?

5 Mike is writing an email to Lisa about what people gave Bob for his trip. Read the sentences in activity four and fill in the missing words about who gave what to Bob, like in the example:

Atkúku kiŋ Bob thiyóblečha waŋ k'ú.

4 Bob and Mike are talking about what people gave to Bob. Can you finish the rest of what Bob and Mike are saying? Fill in the missing words.

Mike: Nihúŋ kiŋ táku _____ he?

Bob: Iná míla kiŋ lé _____ .

Mike: Nithúŋkašila kiŋ táku _____ he?
Bob: Kaká hoíčhuwa kiŋ lé _____ .

Mike: Nikȟúŋši kiŋ táku _____ he?
Bob: Uŋčí watháŋ kiŋ lé _____ .

Mike: Nilékši kiŋ táku _____ he?
Bob: Lekší wíkȟaŋ kiŋ lé _____ .

Iyáyeya	Iȟpéya	Égnaka

From:	Mike
To:	Lisa
Subject:	Bob's going fishing, too!

Hau Lisa,

Atkúku kiŋ Bob thiyóblečha waŋ k'ú.
Bob húŋku kiŋ Bob _____ waŋ _____ .
_____ kiŋ Bob _____ _____ k'ú.
_____ kiŋ Bob _____ _____ ____.
_____ _____ Bob _____ _____ ____.

Tókša akhé,
Mike

6 Read the sentences below. Circle the person who is the giver. Make a square around the person who is the receiver. Underline the thing which was given. Follow the model:

(Bob atkúku kiŋ) [Bob] thiyóblečha waŋ k'ú.

A) Matȟó tȟuŋwíŋču kiŋ Matȟó wihíŋpaspa eyá k'ú.

B) Matȟó tȟuŋkášila kiŋ Matȟó hoíčhuwa waŋ k'ú.

Č) Matȟó lekšítku kiŋ Matȟó thiyóblečha waŋ k'ú.

E) Matȟó húŋku kiŋ Matȟó owíŋža eyá k'ú.

G) Mike Bob owíŋža waŋ k'ú.

H) Mike Bob waglúla eyá k'ú.

I) James Bob hoípatȟe waŋ k'ú.

7 Look at the picture and fill in the missing word in the sentence. Then, fill in the missing part of the verbs, using **ma** or **ni**.

 Iná _____ kiŋ lená ____k'ú.

 Čhiyé _____ kiŋ lé ____k'ú.

 Nilékši kiŋ _____ waŋ ___č'ú.

 Nitȟúŋkašila kiŋ _____ waŋ __č'ú.

 Niyáte kiŋ _____ eyá ____č'ú.

 Nitȟúŋwiŋ kiŋ _____ kiŋ lená ___č'ú.

8 Listen to Matȟó and James. Now, every time you hear the characters say "**nič'ú,**" snap your fingers. Can you catch it every time?

9 Your teacher will give some flashcards to everyone in the class.

Don't show your card or say what it is!

When the class is sitting in a circle, choose someone across the room and give your card to them.

When the person to your left gets a card, ask them what they were given, like in the model.

Joey, táku nič'ú he?

Haŋpóšpula waŋ mak'ú.

10

Step 1:
Find a partner to work with. On a piece of scrap paper, draw six items that you know how to say in Lakota. Cut or tear them apart. Each partner takes three of them.

Step 2:
When the teacher asks you to, choose two or three people to give your drawings to. Don't give any drawings to your partner! You will also receive drawings.

Step 3:
Work with your partner. Show each other what you got. Ask your partner who gave him/her the presents, like in the model below.

Tuwá ... (wówapi) ... kiŋ lé nič'ú he?

(Peter) ... (wówapi) ... kiŋ lé mak'ú.

11 🔊 Listen to the children speaking about who they called.
Draw an arrow from the person who called to the person that they called.

12 Based on the previous listening activity, answer the following questions:

A) James Kimi mas'ákipȟa he?   Háŋ   Hiyá

B) Bob Lisa mas'ákipȟa he?   Háŋ   Hiyá

Č) Kimi Summer mas'ákipȟa he?   Háŋ   Hiyá

E) Matȟó Mike mas'ákipȟa he?   Háŋ   Hiyá

G) Tȟašína Lisa mas'ákipȟa he?   Háŋ   Hiyá

13 Based on your answers to the listening activity write sentences about who called whom. Like this:

James Kimi mas'ákipȟe.

_____

_____

_____

_____

_____

_____

_____

14

a Pretend that one or more of the children from the book have called you.

Your teacher will give you a role play card. It will tell you **who** called you and **when** he/she called.
Your partner will ask you **who** called you, like this:

> Tuwá mas'áničipȟa he?

> (Čhažé) mas'ámakipȟe.

Now ask your partner **who** called him/her!

b Use the same role play card and ask your partner **when** the people called him:

> Tóhaŋ (Čhažé) mas'áničipȟa he?

> (Čhažé) (time) mas'ámakipȟe.

15

Abléza po!

Look at the verbs below and pay attention to whether or not "k" sounds change when **ni** is inserted. Then answer the questions below:

k'ú →	nič'ú
mas'ákipȟa	mas'áničipȟe
waŋyáŋkA	waŋníyaŋke
ókiya	óničiye
khíza	ničhíze
khuwá	ničhúwa
naȟ'úŋ	ničígleğe
ayúta	naníȟ'uŋ
theȟíla	aníyuta
kȟÁ	theníȟila
wók'u	ničhé
kigléğA	wónič'u

How does kh change after **ni**?: _____
How does kȟ change after **ni**?: _____
How does k' change after **ni**?: _____
How does k change after **ni**?: _____

16

First, look at the "me" forms of the verbs below. Underline the part that means "me".

Then, re-write these into the "you" form, like the example. Afterwards, check with your partner.

mas'ámakipȟe ___mas'áničipȟe___

mak'ú _____

napé mayúze _____

themáȟila _____

wómak'u _____

makígleğe _____

yuš'íŋyemaye _____

waŋmáyaŋke _____

makhíze _____

ómakiye _____

omále _____

makhúwa _____

makȟé _____

omáyuspe _____

makhúte _____

aímaȟat'e _____

makípazo _____

amáčhaŋzeke _____

amápȟe _____

17 (a) Here are some items that the children will use to go fishing and hunting with their parents and grandparents! Can you write in the words that are missing? Hint: look back to page 18 if you don't remember them all!

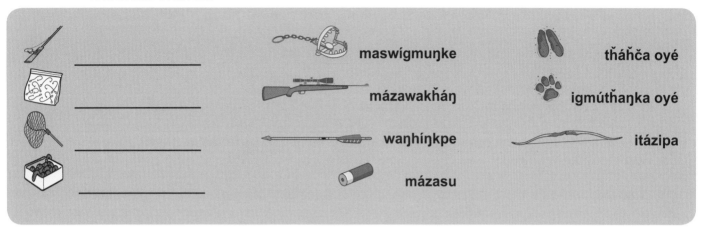

maswígmuŋke

mázawakȟáŋ

waŋhíŋkpe

mázasu

tȟáȟča oyé

igmútȟaŋka oyé

itázipa

(b) Bob and Lisa both want to go fishing and hunting with their parents! But first, they need to learn how to talk about these activities in Lakota. Can you help them? Look up the verbs to the right in your dictionary, and draw lines to match them with the best picture. Some verbs may match more than one picture!

khuwá	gmúŋkA	šutȟÁ
napȟÁ	kigléǧA	hokhúwa
ómna	khuté	wakhúl yÁ
otȟápȟA	ó	waákhita

(č) What do you use to go fishing? How about to go hunting? Use the pictures to make sentences, like the model. Then, check your sentences with a partner.

Howákhuwa čháŋna hočhuwa ilágwaye.

1) _____

2) _____

3) _____

4) _____

5) _____

6) _____

18

A) Skim through the comic strip and figure out the answer to these questions:
Write your answer in the blank.

1) Bob atkúku kičhí hokhúwapi naíŋš wakhúl yápi he? _____

Now read the next two questions, and skim through the comic strip to find the answers.
Write the answers on a piece of scrap paper.
2) Táku wamákȟaškaŋ wičhákhuwapi he?
3) Bob táku wamákȟaškaŋ waŋyáŋka he?

B) Now, skim through the comic again and circle the verbs that have "**ni**" in them.
How many did you find? _____

Write the he/she form of the verbs you circled on a piece of scrap paper. Check with a partner!

Bob: Até kičhí wakhúl uŋyáŋpi.
Waglékšuŋ wičhúŋkhuwapi.

Bob: Mawáni yuŋkȟáŋ igmútȟaŋka waŋ waŋbláke.
Mike: Igmútȟaŋka kiŋ íŋš waŋ**ni**yaŋka he?
Naíŋš na**ni**ȟ'uŋ he?

Bob: Hiyá, waŋmáyaŋke šni, čhaŋkhé čháŋ
waŋ ilázata ináwaȟme.

Mike: Igmútȟaŋka kiŋ ónimna he?
Bob: Háŋ, ómamna yélakȟa.

Mike: **Ni**čhúwa he?
Bob: Háŋ, líla makhúwa, čhaŋkhé paŋȟyá nawápȟe.

Mike: Átaš wókȟokipȟe!!! Iyá**ni**ȟpaya he?
Bob: Háŋ, iyámaȟpaye.

Mike: **Ni**yáȟtaka he?
Bob: Hiyá, mayáȟtake šni, éyaš istó mayúȟlate.

Mike: Tuwá ó**ni**čiya he?
Bob: Áte ómakiye. Oyé otȟámapȟa yuŋkȟáŋ igmútȟaŋka kiŋ khuté na ó.

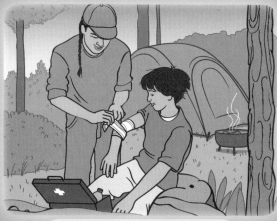

Mike: Tuwá istó **ni**yúwi he?
Bob: Áté istó mayúwi.

Č) Are these sentences right (**Wówičakȟe**) or wrong (**Wówičakȟe šni**)?

1. Bob atkúku kičhí maštíŋčala wičhákhuwapi.
2. Bob matȟó waŋ waŋyáŋke.
3. Igmútȟaŋka waŋ Bob waŋyáŋke.
4. Bob igmútȟaŋka kiŋ oyé otȟápȟe.
5. Bob igmútȟaŋka kiŋ ó.
6. Igmútȟaŋka kiŋ Bob istó yuȟláte.
7. Bob atkúku kiŋ istó yuwí.

19 What other questions do you think the deer asked his friend? Write the answers to the deer's questions. Remember that some letters change after "**ni**".

Naníȟ'uŋpi he?

Háŋ, namáȟ'uŋpi.

Háŋ, makhútepi.

Háŋ, amáyutapi.

Hiyá, maópi šni.

Hiyá, ómamnapi šni.

Háŋ, šumátȟapi.

Hiyá, otȟámapȟapi šni.

Hiyá, makhúwapi šni.

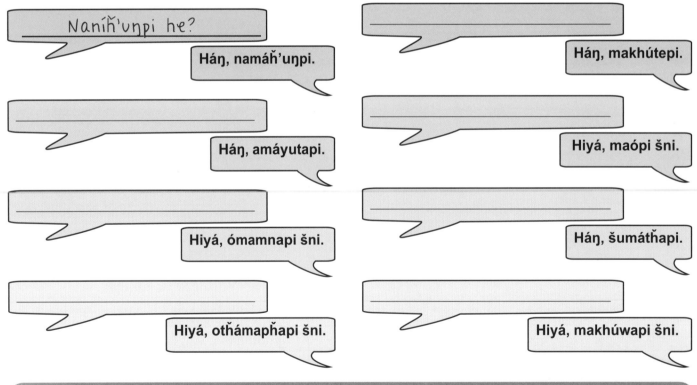

Abléza po!

20 Which of the verbs in each pair tell us that more than one person is doing the activity? Circle the letters.

waŋníyaŋke | waŋníyaŋkapi

waŋmáyaŋke | waŋmáyaŋkapi

21 Here are three stories! Can you figure out how each one goes, using the comic strip to help you? For each story, number the sentences in the correct order, according to what happens in the comic strip.

a
__ Tȟáȟča kiŋ ópi na pȟátapi.

_2_ Tȟáȟča oyé eyá waŋyáŋkapi.

_1_ Wakȟúl yápi kiŋ waákhitapi.

__ Yuŋkȟáŋ táku waŋ naȟ'úŋpi.

__ Wakȟúl yápi kiŋ waŋží tȟáȟča kiŋ khuté.

__ Tȟáȟča waŋ waŋyáŋkapi.

b
__ Wakȟúl yápi kiŋ waŋží tȟáȟča kiŋ khuté.

__ Tȟáȟča kiŋ napȟé.

__ Tȟáȟča oyé eyá waŋyáŋkapi.

__ Wakȟúl yápi kiŋ táku waŋ naȟ'úŋpi.

__ Tȟáȟča kiŋ šutȟé. Ó šni.

č
__ Uŋgnáhaŋla igmútȟaŋka waŋ waŋyáŋkapi.

__ Tȟáȟča oyé eyá waŋyáŋkapi.

__ Wakȟúl yápi kiŋ táku waŋ naȟ'úŋpi.

__ Igmútȟaŋka kiŋ tȟáȟča kiŋ khuwá.

__ Tȟáȟča kiŋ napȟé na igmútȟaŋka kiŋ héčhena ločhíŋ.

27

22 In the comic strips, can you find all of the words where more than one person is doing an activity? Write them below. (Hint: There are 5 of them!). Then, write the dictionary form for each word. If there are some you can't do, you can check in your dictionary!

Form in the story: Dictionary form:

1. _____yápi_____   _____yÁ_____

2. _____   _____

3. _____   _____

4. _____   _____

5. _____   _____

23 a With a partner, choose one of the three stories. Repeat it out loud with each other. Act out the scenes as you talk! Let your teacher know when you can say all the sentences without looking back in your book.

b Now, you and your partner will tell and act out the story to the class! The class will guess which story you are telling, a, b or č. Make sure all of you keep your books closed while you are telling stories.

24 Can you figure out what happened next? Look at the images and sentences below, and match them with the three stories on page 27. Number each image according which of the three stories it matches.

Thiyáta akhípi na tȟaló kiŋ pusyápi na yútapi. Naháŋ tȟahá kiŋ kpaŋyáŋpi.

Tȟáȟča kiŋ wakpála waŋ apsíčiŋ na čhaŋyátakiya íŋyaŋke.

Igmútȟaŋka kiŋ tȟáȟča kiŋ kigléǧiŋ na kté.

25 Choose five of the pictures from the stories on the previous page, and write your own story. Write the five sentences on a piece of scrap paper.

Aŋ

Aŋpétu waŋ él waŋblí waŋ waŋbláke.

26 Say the Lakota "a"
Now try to say it again, but this time move the sound to your nose. Listen to your teacher or a recording and copy the sound.

• Underline the nasal vowels and try saying these words out loud:

áŋpa, háŋpa, waŋblí, čháŋ, sáŋ, káŋ, páŋ, háŋ, waŋží

• Now, read the sentence to the left out loud. Can you say all the "**aŋ**" sounds perfectly?

Iŋ

Wíŋyaŋ kiŋ hé siŋtéȟla kiŋ hé yuš'íŋš'iŋ.

27 Say the Lakota "i."
Now try to say it again, but this time move the sound to your nose. Listen to your teacher or a recording and copy the sound.

• Underline the nasal vowels and try saying these words out loud:

íŋyaŋ, wíŋyaŋ, íŋkpa, híŋhaŋni siŋtéȟla, hiŋháŋ, pȟahíŋ, owíŋ

• Read the sentence out loud. Can you say all the "**iŋ**" sounds pefectly?

Uŋ

Šúŋka k'uŋ hé huŋyákȟuŋ k'uŋ hená úŋ.

28 Say the Lakota "u."
Now try to say it again, but this time move the sound to your nose. Listen to your teacher or a recording and copy the sound.

• Underline the nasal vowels and try saying these words out loud:

šúŋka, itȟúŋkala, uŋčí, huŋyákȟuŋ, osúŋ, úŋšila

• Read the sentence out loud. Can you say all the "**uŋ**" sounds pefectly?

29 Divide the class into teams. Your teacher will say one word from these pairs, and your team needs to vote on whether the words had a nasal vowel or not. If your team votes correctly, you get a point.

A AŊ

ská	skáŋ
čha	čháŋ
ká	káŋ
yašká	yaškáŋ
kȟáta	kȟáŋta
tȟahá	tȟaŋháŋ

I IŊ

hí	híŋ
owáčhi	owáčhiŋ
uŋčí	uŋčhíŋ
kičhí	kičhíŋ
čhičhá	čhiŋčá
čhiyé	čhiŋyé

U UŊ

kú	kúŋ
úpi	úŋpi
sú	súŋ
uŋk'úpi	uŋk'úŋpi
uŋkíyuǧaŋpi	uŋkíyuǧapi
umá	uŋmá

30 Listen to the pairs of words. Number the words in the order that you hear them.

á	áŋ
í	íŋ
ú	úŋ
ská	skáŋ
iyútȟa	iyútȟaŋ
ničhípi	ničhíŋpi
k'ú	k'uŋ
tuwá	tuŋwáŋ
wayáka	waŋyáŋka
há	háŋ
ká	káŋ

Review Quiz

1 Can you match these questions and answers? Draw a line from the question to the best answer.

1. Niyáte kiŋ táku nič'ú he?
2. Nihúŋ kiŋ thiyóblečha waŋží nič'ú he?
3. Tuwá thiyóblečha kiŋ lé nič'ú he?
4. Lisa hoíčhuwa kiŋ lé nič'ú he?
5. Nithúŋkašila watháŋ kiŋ lé nič'ú he?
6. Tuwá wihíŋpaspa kiŋ lená nič'ú he?

a. Thiyóblečha kiŋ lé haŋkáši mak'ú.
b. Hiyá, watháŋ kiŋ lé lekší mak'ú.
č. Até míla waŋ mak'ú.
e. Wihíŋpaspa kiŋ lená tȟaŋké mak'ú.
g. Hiyá, iná owíŋža waŋ mak'ú.
ǧ. Háŋ, hoíčhuwa kiŋ lé mak'ú.

2 Read the sentences below. Circle the person who is the giver. Underline the thing which was given.

a. Matȟó Bob owíŋža waŋ k'ú.
b. Bob Matȟó tȟaŋkéku kiŋ hoíčhuwa waŋ k'ú.
č. Mike čhiyéku kiŋ wíkȟaŋ waŋ k'ú.
e. Summer Lisa paílepi waŋ k'ú.
g. Mike Matȟó hoíyupsiče waŋ k'ú.
ǧ. Tȟašína Kimi thiyóblečha waŋ k'ú.

3 Using the information from exercise 2, write the name of the person who received each of these gifts next to the gift.

_____ _____ _____ _____ _____ _____

4 Here are a series of text messages between Mike and Summer. Can you put them in the right order?

__1__Summer: Ȟtálehaŋ tókhiya yaí he?
_____Summer: Ták tókȟanuŋ he? Nayápȟa he?
_____Mike: Matȟó waŋ é na matȟó čhiŋčála yámni waŋwíčhablake.
_____Mike: Háŋ, waŋmáyaŋkapi čha nihíŋmičiye.
_____Mike: Háŋ, até ómakiye. Matȟó kiŋ napȟé-wičhaye.
_____Summer: Niyáte óničiya he?
_____Mike: Hiyá, nawápȟe šni. Čháŋ waŋ ilázata ináwaȟme.
_____Mike: Héčhel waŋmáyaŋkapi šni, éyaš ómamnapi.
_____Mike: Até kičhí wakhúl uŋyáŋpi.
_____Summer: Matȟó kiŋ waŋníyaŋkapi he?

5 Can you write the correct forms? Change each of the dictionary forms below based on the example:

theȟíla themáȟila theníȟila

kú	ókiyA	waŋyáŋkA
wók'u	mas'ákipȟA	olé
yuš'íŋyeyA	kiyúǧaŋ	oyúspA

1 Matȟó's older brother, Sam, is going to Bear Butte. Why is Sam going? Read part of Lisa and Summer's messaging to find out why! Then, answer the questions about Sam's trip.

March 17th, 8:00 am

Lisa256: Sam tákuwe iyáya he? Slolyáya he?

SummerGirl9: Matȟó čhiyéku kiŋ Sam ečíyapi. Waŋná waníyetu akézaptaŋ čha haŋbléčheya čhíŋ.

Paháta yíŋ kte. Héčhiya aŋpétu tób na haŋhépi tób pahá waŋ akáŋl nážiŋ kte. Pahá kiŋ lé Matȟó Pahá eyápi.

Héčhiya Sam wótiŋ kte šni. Wayátkiŋ kte šni. Éeye lowáŋ na wačhékiyiŋ kte. Wóihaŋble waŋží apȟé kte.

1. Matȟó čhiyéku kiŋ waná waníyetu tóna he?

2. Tókhiya yíŋ kta he?

3. Tákuwe héčhiya yíŋ kta he?

4. Aŋpétu na haŋhépi tóna héčhiya nážiŋ kta he?

5. Sam pahá waŋ akáŋl yaŋkíŋ kte kiŋ hé táku eyápi he?

6. Táku čha apȟé kta he?

7. Wótiŋ kta he?

8. Wayátkiŋ kta he?

2 Cover the dialogue below with a piece of scrap paper and listen to Matȟó's older brother, Sam, talking to his grandfather about his vision quest. What things is his grandfather going to give him to take up the hill? Circle the items.

Wíyaka waŋží mayák'u kta he?

Háŋ, wíyaka waŋží čhič'ú kte.

Sam: Owíŋža waŋží mayák'u kta he?

G: Háŋ, owíŋža waŋží čhič'ú kte.

Sam: Haŋpíkčeka etáŋ mayák'u kta he?

G: Hiyá, haŋpíkčeka tákuni čhič'ú kte šni.

Sam: Wasná etáŋ _____ kta he?

G: Háŋ, wasná etáŋ čhič'ú kte.

Sam: Ptepȟá waŋží mayák'u kta he?

G: Háŋ, ptepȟá waŋ _____ kte.

Sam: Pȟežíȟota etáŋ _____ kta he?

G: Háŋ, pȟežíȟota etáŋ _____ kte.

Sam: Wačháŋǧa etáŋ mayák'u kta he?

G: Háŋ, wačháŋǧa etáŋ čhič'ú kte.

Sam: Čháŋčheǧa waŋží _____ kta he?

G: Háŋ, čháŋčheǧa waŋ _____ kte.

Sam: Ičábu waŋží mayák'u kta he?

G: Háŋ, ičábu waŋží čhič'ú kte.

Sam: Mní etáŋ _____ kta he?

G: Hiyá, mní tákuni _____ kte _____.

3 Uncover the dialogue and listen again. Write in the missing **mayák'u** or **čhič'ú**.

4 Abléza po!

Use these words and fill them in the blanks: you, he/she, I, me, him/her.

k'ú _he/she_ gave it to _him/her_ .

mak'ú _____ gave it to _me_ .

mayák'u _____ gave it to _____ .

nič'ú _he/she_ gave it to _____ .

čhič'ú _I_ gave it to _____ .

5 Matȟó is listening to Sam and his grandfather, and making some notes so he can remember! Can you help him? Write sentences about what Sam's grandfather is going to give him, or will not give him, like the example.

Sam tȟuŋkášitku kiŋ owíŋža _waŋ_ k'ú _kte_ .

Sam tȟuŋkášitku kiŋ haŋpíkčeka _waŋžíni_ k'ú _kte_ _šni_ .

_____

_____

_____

_____

_____

_____

6 Lisa is drawing comics for her younger cousins to show them how to share. Help her fill in the speech bubbles! Choose which speech bubble to fill with **mayák'u kta he?** and which with **čhič'ú kte.**

Wígli-uŋ-káǧapi etáŋ mayák'u kta he?

Háŋ, wígli-uŋ-káǧapi eyá čhič'ú kte.

_____ _____ _____ _____ he?

Háŋ, _____ kte.

Aǧúyapsaka etáŋ _____ kta he?

Háŋ, aǧúyapsaka eyá _____ kte.

_____ he?

Háŋ, _____ kte.

Bloókpaŋla ____ _____ _____ he?

Háŋ, bloókpaŋla _____ _____ kte.

_____ he?

Háŋ, _____ kte.

7 Pretend that you are camping, too! You are in charge of one job at the campsite. Your teacher will give you a card. It will tell you your job, what items you need and what items you have. Ask the other students in your group what they will give you. They will ask you what you will give them.

your job:
you have:
you need:

8 Mike played an important basketball game last week. So he is asking his friends if they saw him play. Listen and check who DID see him.

Lisa, tȟabškátapi kiŋ ektá waŋmáyalaka he?

Háŋ, waŋčhíyaŋke.

Lisa   Tȟašína   Bob   Matȟó

10 Abléza po!

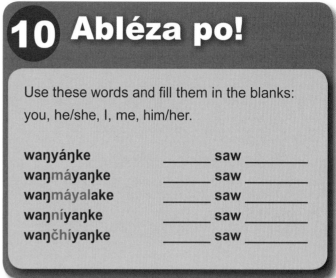

Use these words and fill them in the blanks: you, he/she, I, me, him/her.

waŋyáŋke	_____ saw _____
waŋmáyaŋke	_____ saw _____
waŋmáyalake	_____ saw _____
waŋníyaŋke	_____ saw _____
waŋčhíyaŋke	_____ saw _____

9 Listen again and fill in the proper questions and replies that Mike and his friends make.

Lisa, tȟabškátapi kiŋ ektá waŋmáyalaka he?

Háŋ, waŋčhíyaŋke.

Hiyá, waŋčhíyaŋke _____.
Tȟabškátapi kiŋ ektá waí šni.

Háŋ, _____.
Líla yuphíya tȟabyáškate.

_____, ektá waí šni čha waŋčhíyaŋke šni.

11 The class will divide into two teams. Each team forms two lines facing the opposite team, like in the diagram below.

Now, each person will select someone to ask: Do you see me? You should answer correctly, depending on where you're standing, like in the example. The team with the most correct answers wins!

David, waŋmáyalaka he?

Háŋ, waŋčhíyaŋke.

Jill, waŋmáyalaka he?

Hiyá, waŋčhíyaŋke šni.

→
Direction facing

←
Direction facing

12

Imagine that you and your classmates are animals! Your teacher will give you a card with a picture of your animal. The other students will pretend to be other animals. Ask three of them whether or not they will catch you, and find out what animal they are!

> Matȟó hemáčha. Omáyaluspiŋ kta he?

> Hiyá, itȟúŋkala hemáčha. Očhíyuspiŋ kte šni.

> Háŋ, heȟáka hemáčha. Očhíyuspiŋ kte.

13 Abléza po!

a Look at how these **Y-stem verbs** change to say "*you*." Can you write the correct form?

yuhá -- > luhá "YOU had it"
waŋyáŋkA --> waŋláke "YOU saw him/her/it"

How do the verbs below change to say "*YOU*"?

ayúptA _____
ayúta _____
yuȟíčA _____
ayúštaŋ _____
oyákA _____
oyúspA _____

b Notice how the verb **olúspe** '*you caught him*' changes when we say:
"YOU caught ME" - **omáyaluspe**.

Notice it again on the verb **luȟíče**:
"YOU woke ME" - **mayáluȟiče**.

What letter does **maya** go before when you want to say "*you caught ME*"?

Write it here: _____

14

a Now look at these y-stem verbs. Can you make the same change for them?

waŋláke '*you saw him*' ⟶ _waŋmáyalake_

1) **awáŋlake** ⟶ _____
'you looked after him' 'you looked after me'

4) **alúštaŋ** ⟶ _____
'you left him alone' you left me alone'

2) **alúpte** ⟶ _____
'you answered him' 'you answered me'

5) **waŋláke** ⟶ _____
'you saw her' 'you saw me'

3) **alúta** ⟶ _____
'you were looking at her' 'you were looking at me'

6) **oláke** ⟶ _____
'you told on him' 'you told on me'

b Now let's do this out loud! Close your books. The teacher will give you a verb form. You say the other form back to him/her.

> Waŋláke.

> Waŋmáyalake!

15 **ⓐ** Listen to Matȟó's grandma. She is telling you about the trickster Iktómi, who always does mean things to people and animals. Then, she asks you what each animal says to Iktómi. Can you finish the sentences that the animals say? First, listen and write the answers for each animal.

Iktómi matȟó waŋ yuȟíče. Matȟó kiŋ táku eyá he?
Matȟó kiŋ heyé: "Iktó, mayáluȟičè ló. Amáyuštaŋ yo," eyé.

Iktómi pȟeháŋ waŋ naȟtáke. Pȟeháŋ kiŋ táku eyá he?
Pȟeháŋ kiŋ heyé: "Iktó, _____ ló/kštó. Amáyuštaŋ yo/ye," eyé.

Iktómi hiŋháŋ waŋ ayúta. Hiŋháŋ kiŋ táku eyá he?
Hiŋháŋ kiŋ heyé: "Iktó, _____ yeló/kštó. _____ yo/ye," eyé.

Iktómi šuŋgmánitu waŋ yaȟtáke. Šuŋgmánitu kiŋ táku eyá he?
Šuŋgmánitu heyé kiŋ: "Iktó, _____ _____. _____ yo/ye," eyé.

Iktómi šuŋǧíla waŋ gnáye. Šuŋǧíla kiŋ táku eyá he?
Šuŋǧíla kiŋ heyé: "_____, _____ _____. _____ _____," eyé.

Iktómi tȟatȟáŋka waŋ apȟé. Tȟatȟáŋka kiŋ táku eyá he?
_____ _____: "_____, _____ ____. _____ _____," eyé.

ⓑ Then, listen again, and answer Matȟó's grandma out loud.

16 Now, everyone is at Bear Butte. Matȟó's grandfather is setting up the camp. He is asking the children (all eight) to help him by bringing him the things he needs. Listen to what Matȟó's grandfather says, and match each child with the item he/she is asked to bring.

17 Now, listen again. Which children forgot to bring the item grandfather asked them for?
Write them here: _____

18 **a** Lots of things happen on this trip to Bear Butte! And sometimes children get into arguments. Read this conversation, and figure out who hit whom!

Write it here: _____ *hit* _____.

Bob: Mike, tákuwe amáyapȟa he?

Mike: Hóȟ , ačhípȟe šni.

Bob: Kaká, Mike amápȟe.

Mike: Hiyá, awápȟe šni.

Grandpa: Mike, Bob ayápȟe-ȟča he?

Mike: Kítaŋla awápȟe.

Grandpa: Apȟé šni yo. Tuwéni waápȟe šni.

b Now, read the other conversations!
Figure out who did what to whom, and draw lines to match.

Bob   Lisa   **apȟé**
Mike   Kimi   **oyáke**
Summer   Bob   **yuȟíče**

Kimi: Summer, tákuwe omáyalaka he?
Summer: Átaš, očhíyake šni.
Kimi: Lalá, Summer omáyake.
Summer: Hiyá, obláke šni.
Grandpa: Summer, Kimi oláke-ȟča he?
Summer: Kítaŋla obláke.
Grandpa: Oyáke šni yo. Tuwéni owíčhayake šni.

Lisa: Mike, tákuwe mayáluȟiča he?
Mike: Hóȟ , čhiyúȟiče šni.
Lisa: Lalá, Mike mayúȟiče.
Mike: Hiyá, bluȟíče šni.
Grandpa: Mike, Lisa luȟíče-ȟča he?
Mike: Kítaŋla bluȟíče.
Grandpa: Yuȟíče šni yo. Tuwéni wayúȟiče šni.

č Now, with two partners, select one of the three conversations you have read. Practice acting it out together! Then, perform it from memory in front of the class.

e With your partner write two more dialogues with two of the verbs below. When you are finished, perform one of them for the class.

ayúta   khuwá
naȟtákA   aíȟat'A
yaȟtákA

To help you out, here are the sentences you need to use to finish the dialogues:

Tuwéni waáyuta šni.
Tuwéni wanáȟtake šni.
Tuwéni wayáȟtake šni.
Tuwéni wičhákhuwa šni.
Tuwéni aíwičhaȟat'e šni.

_____
_____
_____
_____
_____
_____
_____
_____
_____

g Listen to the dialogues your classmates are performing. For each dialogue, draw a picture on scrap paper that shows what everybody is doing.

19 Matȟó's brother, Sam, is wondering who will teach him what he needs to know. He is talking to his father.

Listen to their conversation, and decide whether his father tells Sam that he will teach him or that Sam's uncle will teach him. Check the correct box.

(I will teach you how to cook. -- **Lol'íȟ'aŋpi uŋspéčhičhiyiŋ kte.)**
(He will teach you how to cook. -- **Lol'íȟ'aŋpi uŋspénichiyiŋ kte.)**

	Atkúku	Lekšítku
thiyóbleǧa ithíčaǧapi		
čhaŋkábupi		
čhethípi		
lol'íȟ'aŋpi		✓
hokhúwapi		
šiyótȟaŋka yažópi		

20 Your teacher will give you a card with two activities on it. You can do one. But you must find someone else to teach you the other one! Ask your classmates if they can teach you, like the example. Find someone who can! You know you can teach someone if the activity is listed on your card.

Tȟašína, lol'íȟ'aŋpi uŋspémayakhiyiŋ kta he?

Hiyá, lol'íȟ'aŋpi uŋspéčhičhiyiŋ kte šni.

Wačhípi uŋspémayakhiyiŋ kta he?

Háŋ, wačhípi uŋspéčhičhiyiŋ kte.

I can teach: **wačhípi**
I want someone to teach me: **lol'íȟ'aŋpi**

21 Now, write a report about who will teach you what skill, like in the example:

Janet hokhúwapi uŋspémakhiyiŋ kte.
David lowáŋpi uŋspémakhiyiŋ kte.
Sandra wakšúpi uŋspémakhiyiŋ kte.

22 Two weeks before the camping trip, Grandma said that she wanted to show Matȟó how to collect sage. So, Matȟó went out to the country to learn from Grandma.

Pȟežíȟota etáŋ olé ye.

Čhaŋlí etáŋ yuhá wačhékiya ye.

Čhaŋlí kiŋ waúŋyaŋ ye.

Pȟežíȟota kiŋ yušlášla máni ye.

Pȟežíȟota kiŋ pusyá otkéya ye.

Matȟó and his friends followed Grandma's instructions. Write what they did, don't forget to change to the third person plural, like in the model:

| Pȟežíȟota etáŋ olé ye. | 1. _____Pȟežíȟota eyá olépi._____ |

2. _____   4. _____

3. _____   5. _____

23 🔊 Grandpa is asking you to help! Look at the picture on the top of the next page and listen to the items Grandpa wants you to bring. Fill in the missing word.

1. _____ waŋží makáu wo.   5. _____ waŋží makáu wo.

2. _____ etáŋ makáu wo.   6. _____ etáŋ makáu wo.

3. _____ etáŋ makáu wo.   7. _____ etáŋ makáu wo.

4. _____ waŋží makáu wo.   8. _____ waŋží makáu wo.

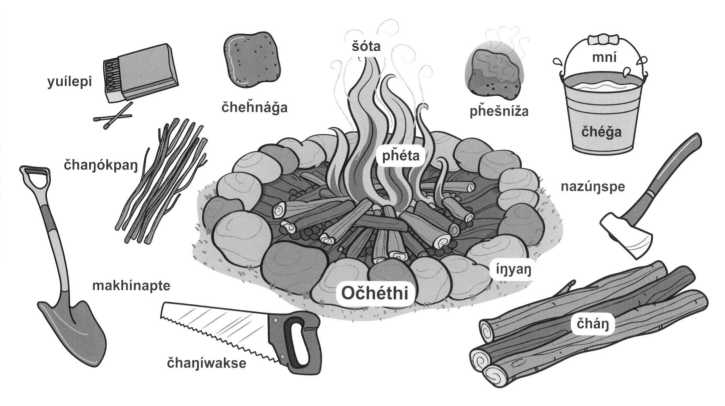

24 **a** You can help Grandpa build a fire!

Look at the pictures and number the commands in the correct order.

Ehákeȟčiŋ čháŋ etáŋ aúŋ wo.

Ho na pȟéta kiŋ awáŋyaŋka yo.

Heháŋl čhaŋókpaŋ etáŋ pahí yo.

1 Tȟokéya očhéthi waŋží káǧa yo.

Heháŋl čháŋ etáŋ kaksáksa yo.

Očhéthi kiŋ iyóhomni íŋyaŋ etáŋ égnaka yo.

Heháŋl čhaŋókpaŋ kiŋ iléya yo.

Heháŋl pȟéta kiŋ póǧaŋ na woíle yo.

b Now, let's act out the steps, like you see in the pictures. Give your partner a command and he/she will perform it.

25 Do you remember each of these activities? Match each sentence with the correct picture by drawing lines. Don't look back at the previous page! See if you can do it from memory.

Mike: **Očhéthi waŋží wakáǧiŋ kte.**

Bob: **Čháŋ etáŋ wakáksaksa kte.**

Tȟašína: **Čhaŋókpaŋ etáŋ wapáhi kte.**

James: **Čhaŋókpaŋ kiŋ iléwayiŋ kte.**

Matȟó: **Pȟéta kiŋ wapóǧaŋ kte.**

Lisa: **Čháŋ etáŋ awáuŋ kte.**

Iyúha: **Pȟéta kiŋ awáŋuŋyaŋkapi kte.**

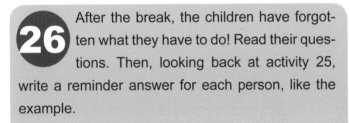

26 After the break, the children have forgotten what they have to do! Read their questions. Then, looking back at activity 25, write a reminder answer for each person, like the example.

1. Mike: **Očhéthi waŋží wakáǧiŋ kte héčha he?**

Háŋ, očhéthi waŋží yakáǧiŋ kte héčha.

2. Lisa: **Čháŋ etáŋ wakáksaksa kte héčha he?**

_____

3. James: **Čhaŋókpaŋ kiŋ iléwayiŋ kte héčha he?**

_____

4. Matȟó: **Čhaŋókpaŋ etáŋ wapáhi kte héčha he?**

_____

5. Bob: **Čháŋ etáŋ awáuŋ kte héčha he?**

_____

6. Iyúha: **Pȟéta kiŋ awáŋuŋyaŋkapi kte héčha he?**

_____

7. Tȟašína: **Pȟéta kiŋ wapóǧaŋ kte héčha he?**

_____

27 a Sam is getting nervous about his vision quest, and is asking Grandpa what to expect. Read the dialogue and draw an X over the things he cannot do or have.

Sam: **Tókheškhe waškáŋ kte héčha he?**
Táku tókȟamuŋ kta he?

Grandpa: **Paháta níŋ kte. Owíŋža nitȟáwa kiŋ akáŋl naŋkíŋ kte. Tákuni yátiŋ kte šni, akíȟ'aŋnič'iyiŋ kte. Tákuni latkíŋ kte šni. Čhaŋnúŋpa kiŋ yuhá wačhéyakiyiŋ kte.**

Sam: **Na heháŋl tókhel waáwakhipȟa kta he?**

Grandpa: **Heháŋl líla loyáčhiŋ kte. Líla ínipuziŋ kte. Íčaťa niȟwá kte. Naháŋ nakéš ništíŋmiŋ kte. Naháŋ uŋgnáš wóihaŋble waŋží waŋlákiŋ kte. Éyaš hé niyé, hé nitȟáwa. Na heháŋl yakú na wóihaŋble kiŋ oyáglakiŋ kte.**

28

Lisa is trying to take some notes about what Sam has to do. Help her organize her notes! Number them in order.

__ kú kte

__ yaŋkíŋ kte

__ tákuni yátiŋ kte šni

__ tákuni yatkíŋ kte šni

__ wačhékiyiŋ kte

__ ločhíŋ kte

__ ípuziŋ kte

__ ȟwá kte

__ ištíŋmiŋ kte

__ wóihaŋble waŋží waŋyáŋkiŋ kte

29

Matȟó's mother is out of town, so he is writing to his mom about the trip after returning. Read his message and answer the questions about the email by circling the correct answer. Be careful - some questions have more than one correct answer!

From: Matȟó

To: Iná

Subject: Sam

Iná, waŋná Sam haŋbléčheya iglúštaŋ. Áta khilí.

Tȟokáheya uŋčí kičhí pȟežíȟota eyá blušlá. Na heháŋl kaká čhethípi uŋspémakhiye. Otȟókaheya thibló kitáŋla nihíŋčiyiŋ na wakȟókipȟe.

Ho éyaš heháŋl blihíč'iye. Kaká pȟežíȟota eyá ičú na pȟaŋkéska waŋ él ognáke.

Yuŋkȟáŋ pȟežíȟota kiŋ iléya čhaŋkhé líla izíte.

Ho na šóta kiŋ uŋ thibló azílye. Heháŋl iníkağapi na heháŋl thibló pahá-ta iyáye.

Héčhiya lowáŋ na wačhékiye.

Tókhe léčhiya yaúŋ ní.

Matȟó

1. **Matȟó tuwá wówapi waŋ kíčağa he?**

   a) **húŋku**   b) **kȟúŋšitku**   č) **čhiyéku**

2. **Sam waŋná táku tókȟuŋ iglúštaŋ he?**

   a) **wól iglúštaŋ**   b) **wayáwa iglúštaŋ**
   č) **haŋbléčheya iglúštaŋ**

3. **Otȟókaheya Matȟó tókhel tȟawáčhiŋ he?**

   a) **nihíŋčiye**   b) **iyókiphi**   č) **čhaŋtéwašte**
   e) **wakȟókipȟe**

4. **Matȟó kȟúŋšitku kiŋ kičhí táku čha yušlá he?**

   a) **wačháŋğa**   b) **pȟežíȟota**   č) **ȟaŋté**

5. **Matȟó tȟuŋkášitku kiŋ táku uŋspékhiya he?**

   a) **hokȟúwapi**   b) **čhethípi**   č) **wakȟútepi**

6. **Matȟó čhiyéku kiŋ tókhiya iyáya he?**

   a) **otȟúŋwahe-ta iyáye**   b) **wayáwa iyáye**
   č) **pahá-ta iyáye**

7. **Héčhiya táku tókȟuŋ he?**

   a) **wóte**   b) **lowáŋ**   č) **wačhí**   e) **wačhékiye**

30  Do you know the difference between **čh** and **č**? Hold your hand in front of your mouth and say **čh** (like English "ch"). Now, try it again, without making the puff of air on your hand, almost like English "j" as in "jam." That's **č**!

 **čhó, čhuwíta, čhuwígnaka, čhóla, čhičhí, čhočhó, čhočhóla**

Ready for more? Read this sentence carefully. Then, try again more quickly, without any mistakes.

Čhápa čhépa waŋ čhaŋmáhel čhéye.

31 Put your hand in front of your mouth again and make the **č** sound (no puff of air). Try some of these words. Say them slowly and carefully, and be careful not to say **čh**! When you can say them slowly, try them again faster.

Č **ičú, čičí, čikčík'ala, čísčila, čočó, čočóla, zičá, théča, héči, uŋčí**

Ready to try something else? Try this sentence, just like the first!

Čičí waŋ čéphaŋši ičú.

32 Now, listen to your teacher or the recording. Your will hear each of the two words - circle the one you hear first!

uŋníčapi | uŋníčhapi	ičáǧe | ičháǧe	uŋkíčupi | uŋkíčhupi
čičí | čhičhí	kíčaǧe | kíčhaǧe	wičákȟa | wičhákȟa
ečékče | ečhékčhe	uŋčí | uŋčhíŋ	wičála | wičhála
hečá | héčha	uŋčíši | uŋčhíši	kíčila | kičhíla
héči | héčhi	uŋkíčaǧapi | uŋkíčhaǧapi	

44

Review Quiz

1 Read the following dialogue and then draw arrows from the person who gave something to what they gave:

Matȟó: Até, Bob kičhí houŋkhuwapi. Hoíčhuwa waŋží mayák'u kta he?

Matȟó Atkúku: Haŋ, čhíŋkš, hoíčhuwa waŋží čhič'ú kte. Éyaš watȟáŋ waníče.

Matȟó: Tókȟa šni. Bob watȟáŋ etáŋ mak'ú kte.

Matȟó Atkúku: Nihúŋ mní etáŋ nič'ú kte . Kilá yo.

Matȟó: Míla waŋží mayák'u kta he, Até?

Matȟó Atkúku: Bob atkúku míla waŋží k'ú he?

Matȟó: Háŋ, Bob atkúku míla waŋ k'ú.

Matȟó Atkúku: Ho ečhá, míš-eyá míla waŋží čhič'ú kte. Oíyokiphi yuhá yo!

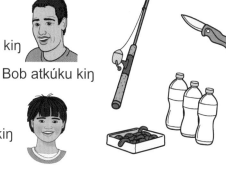

Matȟó atkúku kiŋ

Bob atkúku kiŋ

Matȟó húŋku kiŋ

2 Grandpa is making a fire, and is asking the children to find various things. Draw lines to match them.

Makhínapte waŋží olé po!

Čhéǧa waŋží olé po!

Yuílepi etáŋ olé po!

Nazúŋspe waŋží olé po!

Čhaŋókpaŋ etáŋ olé po!

Íŋyaŋ etáŋ olé po!

Čháŋ etáŋ olé po!

3 Read the following text messages. Decide who is doing the activity. In each line circle the name of the person who did the activity.

Lisa: Háŋ, Tȟašína, wačhípi uŋspéčhičhiyiŋ kte.

Kimi: Háŋ, Tȟašína, Mike kál waŋníyaŋke.

James: Háŋ, Tȟašína, híŋhaŋni kiŋ čhiyúȟičiŋ kte.

Matȟó: Háŋ, Tȟašína, Lisa nignáye.

Mike: Háŋ, Tȟašína, očhíyake.

Summer: Háŋ, Tȟašína, Lisa húŋku awáŋniyaŋkiŋ kte.

4 Can you finish the charts? Fill in the blanks with the correct form of the verb.

I	ablúta		
you (singular)		luhá	
he/she/it			oyáke
you and I	uŋkáyuta		
we			
you (plural)			
they			oyákapi

I	waí		
you (singular)		yak'ú	
he/she/it			ičú
you and I			
we			
you (plural)			
they			

45

1 Let's go to the powwow!
It's Friday, and Bob and Lisa's families are going to the powwow today.

a Bob's mom is telling him which of the family things to take. Listen and circle the things he takes.

b Lisa's father is telling her which of her own things she needs to take. Listen and circle the things that she takes.

> Čhíŋkš, owíŋža kiŋ ičú we.

> Čhúŋkš, owíŋža kiŋ ikíkču wo.

2 Abléza po!

A) Compare these two commands:

Wówapi kiŋ ičú wo/we.
Wówapi kiŋ ikíkču wo/we.

What is different?
Circle the difference.

B) Look at these two Lakota sentences and then answer the questions.

Owíŋža kiŋ ičú wo.
Owíŋža kiŋ ikíkču wo.

• Which of the two sentences tells you to take your own blanket? Circle it.
• Which part of the sentence tells you to take your own blanket? Underline it.

Č) When we see **ikíkču** instead of **ičú**, we know that it is referring to something that belongs to that person. **Ikíkču** is the **possessive** form of **ičú.**

Which of these verbs is **possessive**: **ikíkču** or **ičú**? Write it here: _____

3 Let's pretend you're going to a powwow too! The teacher will tell you what to take to the powwow. Draw what you hear in the correct column, like in the example.

"Oákaŋke kiŋ ičú wo/we."
"Thiyóblečha kiŋ ikíkču wo/we."

My own things   Communal things

5 Tȟašína's mother is asking her if she took **her own** chair. Read the dialogue in activity 6 and answer the questions below.

> Čhúŋkš, oákaŋke kiŋ iyékču he?

> Háŋ, iná, oákaŋke kiŋ iwékču.

A) What is the "I" form of **ikíkču**? _____

B) What is the "you" form of **ikíkču**? _____

6 Read the dialogue between Tȟašína and her mother. Circle the items Tȟašína **already** took.

Mother: Čhúŋkš, háŋpa kiŋ iyékču he?
Tȟašína: Hiyá, iná, háŋpa kiŋ iwékču šni.
Iwékču kte.

Mother: Čhúŋkš, waȟóštaŋ kiŋ iyékču he?
Tȟašína: Hiyá, waȟóštaŋ kiŋ iwékču šni.
Éwektuŋže.

Mother: Čhúŋkš, haŋpóšpula kiŋ iyékču he?
Tȟašína: Háŋ, haŋpóšpula kiŋ iwékču.

Mother: Čhúŋkš, wówapi kiŋ iyékču he?
Tȟašína: Hiyá, wówapi kiŋ iwékču šni.
Owákile kte.

4

1. Put these items on your desk: your own pencil, your own pen, your own book, and your own backpack.

3. If you miss, you must sit down! The last person standing is the winner.

2. Now your teacher will tell you to take **your** pen, or **the** pen; **your** book or **the** book. Take your things ONLY when you hear the right form.

7 🔊

Matȟó and his sister are packing for their trip to the powwow. Listen and circle the items that they already took.

9 In each picture Matȟó has one of **his own** things. Help him say what he has. Write the sentences like in the example.

Haŋpíkčeka kiŋ waglúha

_____

8 🔊 Listen again. Can you fill in all the blanks of the dialogue?

Matȟó: Haŋpíkčeka kiŋ iyékču he?

Sister: Háŋ, haŋpíkčeka kiŋ iwékču.

Sister: Níš tók, haŋpíkčeka kiŋ _____ he?

Matȟó: Háŋ, míš-eyá haŋpíkčeka kiŋ iwékču.

Sister: Ičábu kiŋ iyékču _____?

Matȟó: Tóš ičábu kiŋ iwékču weló.

    Tasé ičábu čhóla mníŋ kte ka!

Matȟó: _____ kiŋ iyékču he?

Sister: Hiyá, naháŋȟčiŋ šiná kiŋ iwékču _____.

    Tókša iwékču kte.

Matȟó: Čhuwígnake kiŋ iyékču he?

Sister: Tóš čhuwígnaka kiŋ _____we.

Matȟó: Wanáp'iŋ kiŋ iyékču he?

Sister: _____ iwékču kte éyaš éwektuŋže.

_____

_____

_____

_____

10

Matȟó's mom is checking up on him, too, to see if he has all of **his** things for the trip. Listen to the dialog and circle the items he says he has.

11

Listen again.
What do you think these phrases mean?

Guess and try to match the translation.

Then check your answer with your partner. Ask the teacher if you're correct.

"Owákile kte ló."   *I will take it (my own).*

"Éwektuŋže ló."   *I will look for it (my own).*

"Iwékču kte."   *I forgot about it.*

12

Work with a partner. Following the example, ask your partner if they have **their own** things with them today. Try using the following items:

mázaškaŋškaŋ, wówapi, wíčazo, wóžuha, wóuŋspe omnáye, itípakhiŋte, hiípažaža, olówaŋ omnáye

Wówapi kiŋ yaglúha he?

Hiyá, wówapi kiŋ waglúha šni. Éwektuŋže.

13 Abléza po!

Take another look at exercise 12 and then answer the questions below.

A) What is the "I" form of **gluhá**?

_____

B) What is the "you" form of **gluhá**?

_____

14 (a)

In each pair of verbs do you know which verbs means *"his/her own"*?

yuhá   ikíkču   pazó

gluhá   ičú   kpazó

(b) Now, underline the part of each verb that means *"his/her own."*

15

Match the verb with its possessive (*his/her own*) form.

ičú

yuhá

yužáža

yútA

yatkÁŋ

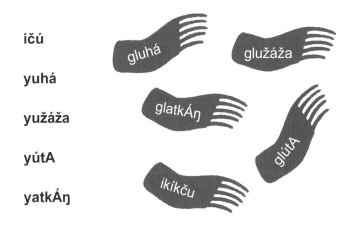

gluhá   glužáža   glatkÁŋ   glútA   ikíkču

By the way, which of the verbs in the activity ablaut? And how do you know?

Wóuŋspe 4

16 Here are some new verbs and their pictures. Can you match them with their possessive forms?

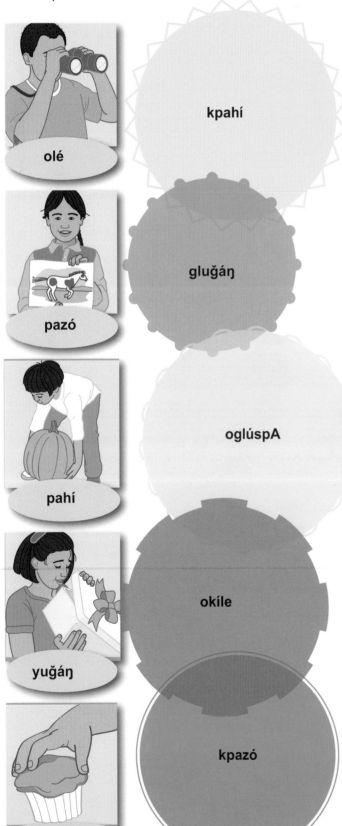

olé

pazó

pahí

yuǧáŋ

oyúspA

kpahí

gluǧáŋ

oglúspA

okíle

kpazó

17 Below are the "*I*" forms of the possessive verbs.

a Can you write the "*he/she*" form of these verbs?

owákile _____

owágluspe _____

wakpázo _____

wakpáhi _____

waglúǧaŋ _____

waglátke _____

waglúte _____

waglúha _____

waglúžaža _____

iwékču _____

b Look at the verbs above again. Can you circle the part of the verb that means "*I*"?

č Which of the "*I*" forms of the verbs is different from the rest?
Write it here: _____

e Divide the class into several teams.
Line up with your team in the back of the room, away from the board. Your teacher will write the "*I*" or "*you*" form of a verb on the board.

One member from each team must run up to the board and write the other form (either "*I*" or "*you*" form) on the board.

The first team that writes the correct answer on the board gets a point!

18 🔊 What sound do you make when you're clearing your throat? Try making the ȟ sound, just like you hear it from your teacher or in the recording.

Ȟ ȟ

When you can make the sound, try to say these words!

ȟé, ȟá, ȟóta, ȟáŋ

No problem? Now, try to say this sentence. Try it the first time very slowly and carefully. Then, try it again a little faster.

Ȟláȟla kiŋ yuȟláȟla na iȟáȟa.

19 🔊 Now try ǧ! Try making the ȟ sound, but make it heavier (voiced), just like you hear it from your teacher or in the recording.

Ǧ ǧ

When you can make the sound, try to say these words!

ǧí, ǧú, ǧáŋ, ǧópA

Do you hear the difference between ȟ and ǧ? Now, try to say this sentence. Try it the first time very slowly and carefully. Then, try it again a little faster.

Aǧúyapi aǧúǧu káǧe.

20 Lisa is describing her grandfather's **regalia**.
Listen and number the items in the order that you hear them.
Check with your glossary and draw a line from the word to the picture. Three lines
have been drawn for you already!

Wókȟoyake

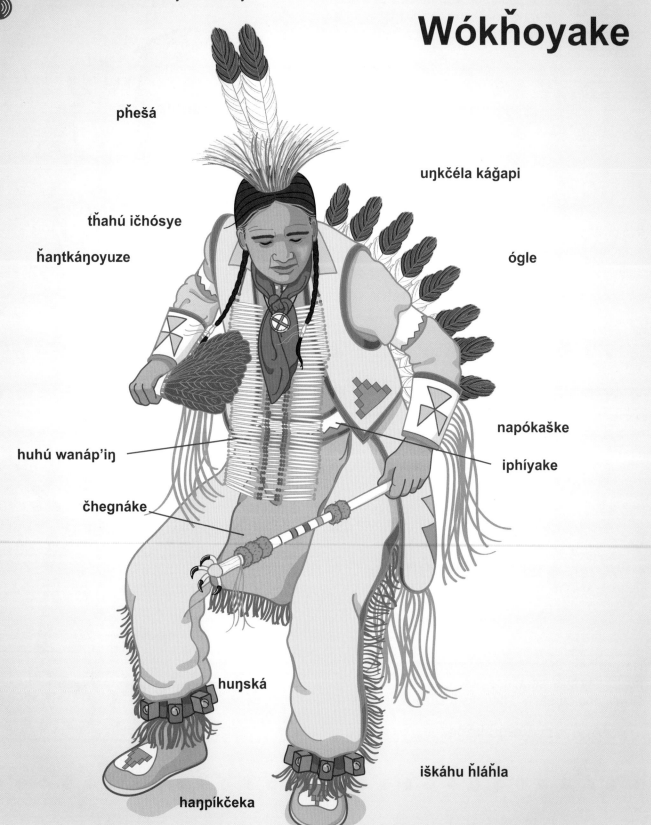

pȟešá

uŋkčéla káǧapi

tȟahú ičhósye

ógle

ȟaŋtkáŋoyuze

napókaške

huhú wanáp'iŋ

iphíyake

čhegnáke

huŋská

iškáhu ȟláȟla

haŋpíkčeka

52

21 **a** Work with your partner. Can you label the things that Lisa's mom is wearing? Check in your dictionary for words you don't know!

b What kind of dancer is Lisa's mom? Write it here: _____. How can you tell?

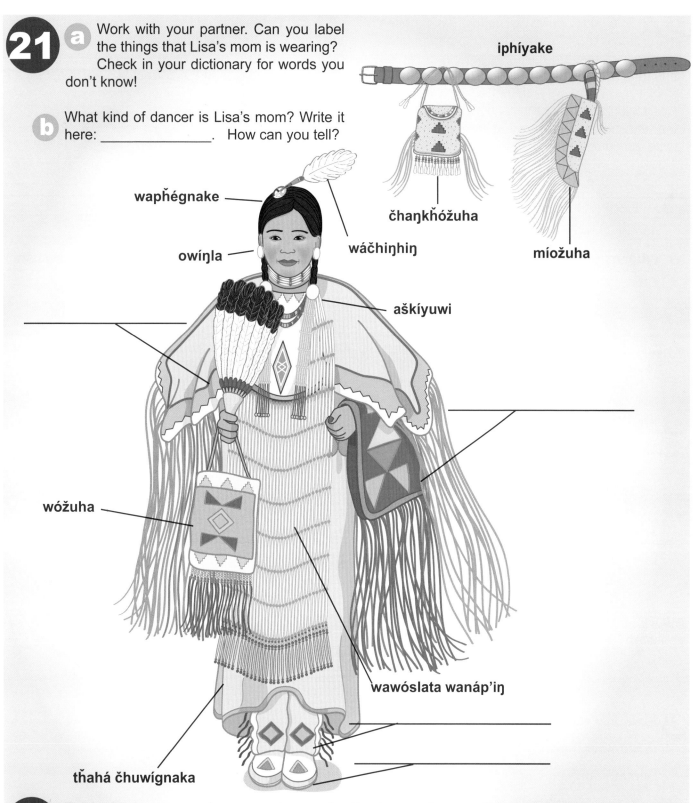

iphíyake

waphégnake

čhaŋkȟóžuha

owíŋla

wáčhiŋhiŋ

míožuha

aškíyuwi

wóžuha

wawóslata wanáp'iŋ

tȟahá čhuwígnaka

22 Think about a man and a woman in your family who are dancers. Take out a piece of scrap paper and draw their regalia. Then, write a description, like the model. If you do not know any dancers, use your imagination.

23 Your partner will describe his/her family member's regalia. Draw what you hear on a piece of scrap paper.

Wóuŋspe 4

24 The kids' powwow things have gotten all mixed up! They are trying to organize everything now. They are talking about their own things, and things that are not their own.

Read the first sentence in each pair. Decide whether the item belongs to the child talking or not. Then, write the correct form of the verb in the blank.

1 Čhaŋógnake kiŋ lé James tȟáwa.

James čhaŋógnake kiŋ lé _____.

(yuǧáŋ / gluǧáŋ)

2 Huŋská kiŋ lé Bob tȟáwa šni.

Bob huŋská kiŋ _____.

(oyúspA / oglúspA)

3 Pȟešá kiŋ lé Mike tȟáwa šni.

Mike pȟešá kiŋ _____. (ičú / ikíkču)

4 Waháčhaŋka kiŋ lená Tȟašína tȟáwa.

Tȟašína waháčhaŋka kiŋ _____.

(olé / okíle)

5 Čháŋčheǧa kiŋ lé Matȟó tȟáwa šni.

Matȟó čháŋčheǧa kiŋ _____.

(iyéye / iyékiye)

6 Šiná úŋ wačhí čhuwígnake kiŋ

lé Summer tȟáwa.

Summer šiná úŋ wačhí čhuwígnake kiŋ

_____. (pazó / kpazó)

7 Haŋpíkčeka kiŋ lé Kimi tȟáwa šni.

Kimi haŋpíkčeka kiŋ _____.

(pahí / kpahí)

25 Listen to what Lisa says about what the other children are holding. Decide whether each child is holding his/her own item, or someone else's. Circle the correct answer in each pair.

 tȟáwa
tȟáwa šni

 tȟáwa
tȟáwa šni

 tȟáwa
tȟáwa šni

 tȟáwa
tȟáwa šni

 tȟáwa
tȟáwa šni

 tȟáwa
tȟáwa šni

26 Can you understand what your partner is telling you to do? Choose and say a command, and your partner will act it out. Try a few commands, then switch.

You should say what you're doing too, like in the example.

> Wíčazo kiŋ kpahí yo!

> Wíčazo kiŋ wakpáhi.

Here are some commands you can try:

Háŋpa kiŋ kpazó wo/we.
Wíčazo kiŋ kpahí yo/ye.
Wówapiska kiŋ ikíkču wo/we.
Wóžuha kiŋ oglúspa yo/ye.
Wóžuha kiŋ gluǧáŋ yo/ye.
Mní kiŋ glatkáŋ yo/ye.
Wóyute kiŋ glúta yo/ye.
Napé kiŋ glužáža yo/ye.

27 The children are doing various activities with their own things at the powwow. Can you fill in the speech bubbles? Choose a different verb for each speech bubble. Don't forget to use the "I" form of the verb!

glatké, glužáža, kpazó, ~~okíle~~, glúte, ikíkču, gluǧáŋ, oglúspe, kpahí

Haŋpíkčeka kiŋ owákile.

28 Lisa and Kimi are eating apples. Read the sentences and decide who is eating her own apple, and who is eating an apple from the cafeteria. Match each sentence to its translation.

> Ťhaspáŋ waŋ wáte.

A) *I am eating some apples*

B) *I am eating an apple.*

C) *I am eating one of my apples.*

> Ťhaspáŋ waŋ waglúte.

A) *I am eating some apples*

B) *I am eating an apple.*

C) *I am eating one of my apples.*

29 Pretend that you're at the powwow and you're hungry! You can choose between the food that you brought and the food that is available for everyone. Choose what you're going to eat and ask your partner what they're going to choose. Follow the models.

> Táku čha yátiŋ kta he?

> _____ kiŋ wátiŋ kte.

-or-

> _____ kiŋ waglútiŋ kte.

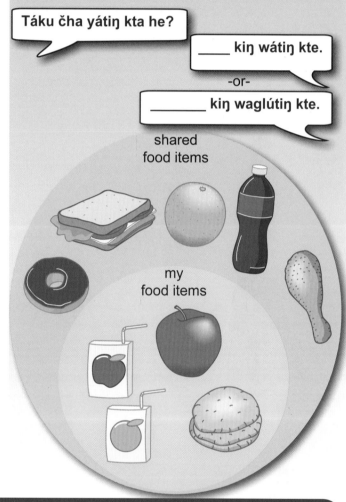

shared food items

my food items

30

a Listen to the narrator ask each child what they ate. Using the picture at the left, match the food item with the child that ate it.

b Based on the listening, decide whether the thing the person ate was their own or shared at the picnic. Circle the food items that were shared.

31 Lisa says "*Tȟašína called ME last night*". Tȟašína says "*I called Lisa*".
Can you help the other children finish their sentences saying who they called?

Tȟašína mas'ámakipȟe.

Bob mas'ámakipȟe.

Kimi mas'ámakipȟe.

Mathó mas'ámakipȟe.

Lisa mas'áwakipȟe.

32 Read my sentences and decide which of the things I did to my friends and which things they did to me. Draw arrows, like in the model.

Kimi owíŋ eyá mak'ú.

James aíwaȟat'e.

Mike wówak'u.

Tȟašína amáyuta.

Mathó waŋbláke.

Lisa omáyuspe.

57

Matȟó líla wačhí kte ȟčiŋ!

1) Waníyetu mašákowiŋ kʼuŋ héhaŋ wačhí akíčhiyapi waŋ él ówapȟa kte ȟčiŋ. Čhaŋkhé wačhí wókȟoyake kiŋ owákile. Pȟeží mignáka wawáčhi.

33 Matȟó needs to get ready for a dance competition. Let's see what happens to him! Follow the directions to do each activity below.

a First, look through the pictures to find out what kind of dancer Matȟó is. Skim through the text to find out how to say it in Lakota.

Write it here: _____

b Next, look at picture #7. What is he looking for?
Write it here: _____

How are you doing? Check your answers with your teacher before going on!

č Can you guess what the word **wagnúni** in picture #7 means? Circle the answer.

A) I have them.
B) I lost them.
C) I forgot them.

e Look through the text and circle all the possessive verbs.

4) Haŋpíkčeka kiŋ oákaŋke háŋska kiŋ ilázata úŋ čha wakpáhi.

7) Iyéčhiŋkiŋyaŋke kiŋ ókšaŋ haŋpíkčeka kiŋ owákile na owákile, éyaš iyéwakiye šni. Wagnúni séče.

2) Haótkeye kiŋ waglúǧaŋ. Huŋská mitȟáwa kiŋ čhaŋóphiye waŋ ogná úŋ, čha iwékču.

3) Ógle mitȟáwa kiŋ šápa čha waglúžaža.

5) Iná heyé: "Ináȟni yo," eyé. Iyéčhiŋkyaŋke kiŋ ogná íblotakiŋ na wókȟoyake kiŋ oglúspa maŋké.

6) Wačhípi kiŋ ektá uŋkípi na heháŋl wókȟoyake kiŋ wéčʼuŋ, éyaš haŋpíkčeka kiŋ waglúha šni. Tókȟaȟʼaŋ.

8) Waȟpé wókheya kiŋ ektá sičhóla waí éyaš, haŋpíkčeka čhóla mawáni čha tókheni wawáčhi šni.

9) Tȟaŋháŋši Mike él mahí, haŋpíkčeka kiŋ glušlókiŋ na omákʼu. Yuŋkȟáŋ heyé: "Níš wačhí yo." eyé.

59

34 True or false? Read Matȟó's story again and circle **háŋ** or **hiyá**.

1) Matȟó huŋská tȟáwa kiŋ čhaŋóphiye akáŋ úŋ.
Háŋ / Hiyá

2) Ógle kiŋ owákšiyužaža mahél glužáža.
Háŋ / Hiyá

3) Haŋpíkčeka kiŋ oákaŋke háŋske kiŋ itȟókab úŋ.
Háŋ / Hiyá

4) Iyéčhiŋkyaŋke kiŋ akáŋl haŋpíkčeka kiŋ okíle.
Háŋ / Hiyá

5) Wókȟoyake kiŋ hakíč'uŋ k'uŋ héhaŋ táku čha yuhá šni.
Háŋ / Hiyá

35 Read the last frame of the comic again. What do you think **omák'u** most likely means? Circle the answer.

A) *He lent them to me.*
B) *He bought them for me.*
C) *He put them on for me.*

36 Let's find out about you and your class-mates at your own powwows! First, take the survey below. Write your answers to each question on a piece of scrap paper.

Wawíyuŋǧapi 1

1) Matȟó wačhí. Níš tók? Níš-eyá wayáčhi he?

2) Matȟó pȟeží mignáka wačhí. Níš wačhípi kiŋ tukté waŋží wayáčhi he?

3) Matȟó wačhí wókȟoyake eyá waštéšte čha gluhá. Níš-eyá wačhí wókȟoyake etáŋ yaglúha he?

37 Now, find two classmates and ask them the same survey questions. Were their answers the same or different?

38 Read through the questions in the second survey. Check the answer that fits you best.

Wawíyuŋǧapi 2

1 Takúŋl wagnúni čháŋna _____ .

a) wačhéye
b) mačháŋzeke
č) owákile
e) kȟáŋmat'e

2 Okȟólawaya waŋží takúŋl gnúni čháŋna _____ .

a) ówakiye
b) aíwahat'e
č) owále
e) wačhéye

3 Mike Matȟó haŋpíkčeka tȟáwa kiŋ ok'ú. Níš ták tókȟanuŋ kta tkȟá he?

a) Haŋpíkčeka kiŋ olé ówakiyiŋ kte.
b) Haŋpíkčeka mitȟáwa kiŋ owák'u kte.
č) Haŋpíkčeka mitȟáwa kiŋ owák'u kte šni, ičhíŋ wawáčhi kte.

39 Now talk to your partner. Read your sentences, and listen to your partner's sentences. Are they the same or different?

Review Quiz

1 Kimi is getting ready to go to the powwow! She has put some things together to take with her. On scrap paper, write sentences to say whether she took her own things, or things belonging to everyone at her house, according to the pictures. Things with a name tag on them belong to her!

2 What are you doing? Pretend that you are the child in each of the pictures. Write sentences about what you are doing with your things, like the model:

Žiškopela waŋ waglúte.

_____

_____

_____

_____

3 Pretend you are Mike! Can you write sentences to say what you are doing to someone else, or what they are doing to you? Use the arrows and the models to help you. Write your sentences on a piece of scrap paper.

Mike----> James (waŋyáŋkA): *James waŋbláke.*

James----> Mike (mas'ákipȟA): *James mas'ámakipȟe.*

a. James ---> Mike (ayúta):
b. Mike ----> Lisa (aíȟat'A):
č. Bob ---> Mike (apȟÁ):
e. Mike ---> Matȟó (wók'u):
g. Summer ---> Mike (oyúspA):
ǧ. Mike ----> Kimi (yuš'íŋyeyA):

4 Can you pick the right verb from the choices? Read the sentence, and then circle the correct verb.

a Wówapi kiŋ lé Kimi tȟáwa šni.
Kimi wówapi kiŋ lé (gluǧáŋ / yuǧáŋ).

b Haŋpíkčeka kiŋ lená James tȟáwa.
James haŋpíkčeka kiŋ lená (oyúspe / oglúspe).

č Wóžuha kiŋ lé Lisa tȟáwa.
Lisa wóžuha kiŋ lé (olé / okíle).

e Ógle kiŋ lé Mike tȟáwa šni.
Mike ógle kiŋ lé (pazó / kpazó).

g Wapȟóštaŋ kiŋ lé Matȟó tȟáwa.
Matȟó wapȟóštaŋ kiŋ lé (ikíkču / ičú).

ǧ Owíŋla kiŋ lé Summer tȟáwa šni.
Summer owíŋla kiŋ lé (yuhá / gluhá).

5 Do you remember all the words for the regalia? Your teacher will give you a blank worksheet to fill in. See how much you can do without looking back at the pictures on pages 52 and 53. When you have done as much as you can on your own, check with a partner. Then check back in the book to see what you missed.

Owáyawa Wótȟaŋiŋ

Aŋpétu kiŋ lé owáyawa ektá wóuŋspe khuwápi kiŋ wíkičhiyuŋǧapi. Táku tókȟuŋ awáštelakapi he? Táku oglákapi he?

REPORTER: Bob, yanúŋwaŋ he?
BOB: Háŋ, óhiŋniyaŋ líglila wanúŋwe s'a.

REP.: Tuktétu čha eyášna yanúŋwaŋ he?
BOB: Blokétu čháŋna šna wakpá waŋží él wanúŋwe, ho na waníyetu čháŋna šna onúŋwe thípi waŋží él wanúŋwe.

REP.: Lisa, níš-eyá yanúŋwaŋ he?
LISA: Háŋ, enána wanúŋwe.

REP.: Wayákšupi he?
BOB: Hiyá, tóhaŋni wawákšu šni.
LISA: Háŋ, watóhaŋlšna wawákšu. Uŋčí wakšúpi uŋspémakhiye.

REP.: Wayáčhi he?
LISA: Líglila wawáčhi. Tuktétu ȟčiŋ wačhípi čháŋna ektá mníŋ na wawáčhi. Líla wačhí awáštewalake.

REP.: Bob, níš tók, wayáčhi he?
BOB: Háŋ, watóhaŋlšna wawáčhi.

REP.: Nakúŋ yalówaŋ he?
BOB: Háŋ, nakúŋ walówaŋ. Ȟ'okȟá hemáčha čha walówaŋ s'a na nakúŋ čhaŋwákabu s'a.
LISA: Háŋ, míš-eyá walówaŋ s'a.

REP.: Wówapi lawápi he?
BOB: Háŋ, óhiŋniyaŋ wówapi blawá.
LISA: Míš-eyá óhiŋniyaŋ wówapi blawá.

1 Lisa and Bob have been interviewed for an article about hobbies! Read through the questions that the reporter asks, and circle the hobbies that he asks about.

2 Read the article and match Bob and Lisa with the hobbies that they do. Be careful! Some activities are done by both.

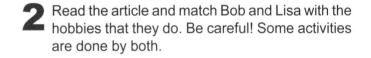

wanúŋwe

wawáčhi

walówaŋ

wawákšu

šuŋk'ákaŋmaŋke

tȟabwáškate

waíŋmnaŋke

wówapi blawá

3 On the left is a graph showing how often activities are done, from "never' to "always". Read through the newspaper article again. For each person, write the name of the activity in the correct place next to the graph. Here is an example of Summer's activities, which are not in the article you read.

	Summer	Bob	Lisa
tóhaŋni ... šni			
enána	wawáčhi		
watóhaŋlšna			
s'a	wawákšu		
óhiŋniyaŋ	waíŋmnaŋke		

4 Abléza po!

Now, work with a partner. Look back at the article. Can you find and circle all the words that are "you" forms of verbs? Some verbs repeat.

Now, can you underline the letters in each of the verbs that mean "you"?

5 Read the article again and answer the questions below.

1) Bob waníyetu čháŋna šna tuktél nuŋwáŋ he?

_____

2) Bob blokétu čháŋna šna tuktél nuŋwáŋ he?

_____

3) Tuwá Lisa wakšúpi uŋspékhiya he?

_____

4) Lisa wačhí awáštelaka he?

_____

6 Bob and Lisa were showing their things to the reporter. Now, all their things are in one big pile. Bob and Lisa are identifying their own things. Can you help them finish their sentences, using the information from the interview?

Nuŋwáŋpi hayápi tȟó kiŋ lé mitȟáwa.

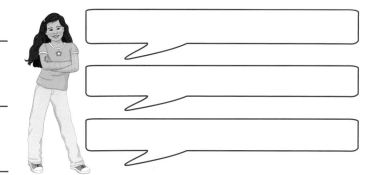

7 🔊 A reporter is interviewing Mike about hobbies. Listen to what he says about himself and his brother, then check off the activities that each one does, like in the model.

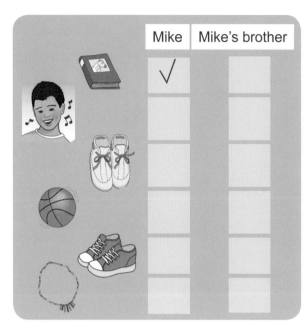

8 **a** Can you finish the questions with the correct letters that mean "you" for each verb? Decide between **ya**, **l** and **n**. Then, write the answers to the questions for yourself, saying how often you do the activity.

MIYÉ	
Ya **núŋwaŋ he?**	Háŋ, watóhaŋlŝna wanúŋwe. / Hiyá, tóhaŋni wanúŋwe ŝni.
Wa_____čhi he?	
_____lówaŋ he?	
Wa_____kšu he?	
Ťhab_____škata he?	
Ya íŋ n aŋka he?	
Šuŋk'ákaŋ___aŋka he?	
Hunáhomnipi akáŋ___aŋka he?	
Wówapi ___awá he?	
Šúŋka waŋží awáŋ___aka he?	
Wamákȟaškaŋ etáŋ wičhá___uha he?	
Ťhaŋ_____gluškehaŋ he?	

b Next, ask three different people. They will also be asking you! Write three sentences about each of the classmates you talk with.

wakšúpi

wówapi yawápi

nuŋwáŋpi

sítȟapa škátapi

wakáǧapi

tȟab'ápȟapi

lowáŋpi

tȟabškátapi

9 Lisa wants to write an article for the school newspaper. Lisa is interviewing her aunt who is a new teacher at the school, to find out what activities she knows how to do.

Lisa: Tȟuŋwíŋ, šuŋk'ákaŋyaŋkapi uŋníspe he?
Aunt: Háŋ, šuŋk'ákaŋyaŋkapi uŋmáspe.

a Number the activities that Lisa mentions as you hear them, like in the example.

b Then listen again, and check if the teacher can do the activity, like in the example.

____ háŋpapȟečȟuŋpi   ____ wakhúl yápi
____ sítȟapa škátapi   ____ wakšúpi
____ khiíŋyaŋkapi   ____ tȟabškátapi
____ wakáǧapi   ____ tȟab'ápȟapi
_1._ šuŋk'ákaŋyaŋkapi ✓
____ nuŋwáŋpi
____ lowáŋpi

10 Can you help Lisa finish writing the article about her aunt? Using the information from exercise nine, write in either **uŋspé** or **uŋspé šni** for each skill, like the example.

Tȟuŋwíŋ tȟabškátapi <u>uŋspé</u>, éyaš tȟab'ápȟapi <u>uŋspé šni</u>.

1. Nakúŋ sítȟapa škátapi _____ .

2. Khiíŋyaŋkapi _____ .

3. Nuŋwáŋpi _____ .

4. Háŋpapȟečȟuŋpi _____ .

5. Wakhúl yápi _____ .

6. Wakšúpi _____ .

7. Lowáŋpi _____ .

8. Wakáǧapi _____ .

11 Now, answer the questions for yourself! Take out a piece of scratch paper and write your answers to the questions, like in the example.

Šuŋk'ákaŋyaŋkapi uŋníspe he?
Háŋ, šuŋk'ákaŋyaŋkapi uŋmáspe.

1. Tȟabškátapi uŋníspe he?
2. Tȟab'ápȟapi uŋníspe he?
3. Sítȟapa škátapi uŋníspe he?
4. Khiíŋyaŋkapi uŋníspe he?
5. Nuŋwáŋpi uŋníspe he?
6. Háŋpapȟečhuŋpi uŋníspe he?
7. Wakhúl yápi uŋníspe he?
8. Wakšúpi uŋníspe he?
9. Lowáŋpi uŋníspe he?
10. Wakáǧapi uŋníspe he?

12 Next, interview your partner and write an article about them, like Lisa wrote about her teacher.

Šuŋk'ákaŋyaŋkapi uŋníspe he?

Háŋ, šuŋk'ákaŋyaŋkapi uŋmáspe. / Hiyá, šuŋk'ákaŋyaŋkapi uŋmáspe šni.

13 Bob is asking his friends what they like to do. Match their response with their picture. Then listen and see if you're correct.

 1 Wakhúl yá awáštewalake.

 2 Wakšú awáštewalake.

 3 Wačhí awáštewalake.

 4 Lowáŋ awáštewalake.

5 Wakáȟ awáštewalake.

 6 Khiíŋyaŋg awáštewalake.

 7 Tȟabškál awáštewalake.

14

Which verb is used in each phrase? Can you match the phrases on the left with the basic form of the verb on the right? Draw lines, like the example:

Ťhabškál awáštewalake.	ťhab'ápȟA
Ťhab'ápȟa awáštewalake.	šuŋk'ákaŋyaŋkA
Síťhapa škál awáštewalake.	khiíŋyaŋkA
Khiíŋyaŋg awáštewalake.	waŋyáŋg yaŋkÁ
Šuŋk'ákaŋyaŋg awáštewalake.	wówapi yawá
Nuŋwáŋ awáštewalake.	háŋpapȟečhuŋ
Háŋpapȟečhuŋ awáštewalake.	ťhabškátA
Wakhúl yá awáštewalake.	lowáŋ
Wakšú awáštewalake	wakhúl yÁ
Lowáŋ awáštewalake	wakšú
Wakáȟ awáštewalake	síťhapa škátA
Waŋyáŋg yaŋká awáštewalake	wakáǧA
Wówapi yawá awáštewalake	nuŋwÁŋ

15 Abléza po!

Look at these examples:

ťhabškátA -- ťhabškál awáštelake
lowáŋ -- lowáŋ awáštelake

Which of the two uses a shortened form of the basic verb before **awaštélakA**?
Circle it.

Now, look at the list of the verbs in exercise 13. Circle all of the ones that use a shortened form. How many did you find?

16

a Write five things that you like to do. Look back at activity 13 for some ideas.

b Now, interview three or more of your classmates and write down some of the things that they like to do. They will interview you, too!

1.

2.

3.

4.

5.

Ťhabškál awášteyalaka he?

Háŋ, ťhabškál awáštewalake.

Hiyá, ťhabškál awáštewalake šni.

č Now, talk about three of the people you interviewed. Take out a piece of scrap paper. Write down some of the things that those three people like to do, like in the model.

Kelly wakáȟ awáštelake.
Gabe šuŋk'ákaŋyaŋg awáštelake šni.

17 Kimi and Tȟašína were interviewed for an article about children's hobbies that appeared in a regional magazine, **Wakȟáŋheža.** Now the girls are famous!

Read through the article from the magazine, and decide whether Kimi, Tȟašína, or both girls do each of the hobbies. Check off the activities, like in the example to the right.

	Kimi	Tȟašína
1. Wayáčhipi he?	✓	
2. Yalówaŋpi he?		
3. Yanúŋwaŋpi he?		
4. Yaíŋnaŋkapi he?		
5. Wayákšupi he?		
6. Tȟabyáškatapi he?		
7. Šuŋk'ákaŋnaŋkapi he?		

INTERVIEWER: Kimi, wayáčhi he?

KIMI: Háŋ, wawáčhi.

INT.: Tȟašína, níš tók, wayáčhi he?

TȞAŠÍNA: Háŋ, míš-eyá wawáčhi s'a.

INT.: Kimi, yaíŋnaŋka he?

KIMI: Hiyá, waíŋmnaŋke šni.

INT.: Tȟašína, níš tók, yaíŋnaŋka he?

TȞAŠÍNA: Háŋ, míš líla waíŋmnaŋke.

INT.: Yalówaŋpi he?

KIMI: Háŋ, wačhípi čháŋna šna walówaŋ s'a.

TȞAŠÍNA: Háŋ, míš-eyá.

INT.: Yanúŋwaŋpi he?

KIMI: Háŋ, uŋnúŋwaŋpi. Mnikȟáta ektá šna uŋnúŋwaŋpi.

INT.: Tȟabyáškatapi he?

TȞAŠÍNA: Háŋ, óhiŋniyaŋ tȟab'úŋškatapi.

INT.: Wayákšupi he?

KIMI: Háŋ, nuphíŋ watóhaŋlšna waúŋkšupi.

INT.: Šuŋk'ákaŋnaŋkapi he?

TȞAŠÍNA: Háŋ, blokétu čháŋna šna nuphíŋ šuŋk'ákaŋuŋyaŋkapi.

18 Abléza po!

Read these two dialogues. What is different about the verb form in the second dialogue? Can you circle it?

1 Kimi, yalówaŋ he?

Háŋ, walówaŋ.

2 Kimi, Tȟašína, yalówaŋpi he?

Háŋ, walówaŋ.

Háŋ, walówaŋ.

So, if we want to ask just one person, "Do you play basketball?" which question should we use? Circle it.

1) Tȟabyáškatapi he?
2) Tȟabyáškata he?

If you are asking more than one person, which question do you use? Circle it.

1) Tȟabyáškatapi he?
2) Tȟabyáškata he?

19 Mike is preparing interview questions for a report he will be doing on other students. Look at the questions he has written down to ask just one person below. Can you help him change his notes so that he can ask more than one person, since he will be interviewing a group of students? Write the new questions on a piece of scrap paper.

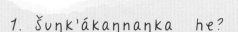

1. Šuŋk'ákaŋnaŋka he?

2. Wayáčhi he?

3. Yaíŋnaŋka he?

4. Yanúŋwaŋ he?

5. Wayákšu he?

6. Yanúŋwaŋ he?

7. Tȟabškál awášteyalaka he?

20 Let's figure out some questions so that you can interview your classmates! Look at the model questions below. Can you write three more questions like the example? Write them on a piece of scrap paper.

Lowáŋ awášteyalakapi he?
Tȟabškál awášteyalakapi he?

22 How do you ask these questions? Look at the activity and how many people you're asking, then write the question below.

a _____ ?

b _____ ?

č _____ ?

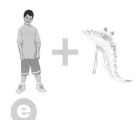

e _____ ?

21 Now, let's interview! Get in groups of four. Write each of your partner's names in the name spaces. Then ask the questions you wrote to the group (do you all like to....?). Check the box for each person in your group who likes each activity.

Čhažé	1	2	3

23

1 🔊 Hold out your hand and try the first word.
Do you feel the puff of air on your hand?

2 🔊 Now, try the second word, but try to say it without the puff of air.

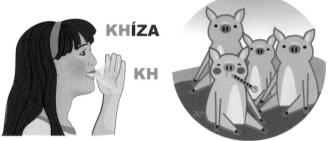

KHÍZA

KH

KÍZA

K

KH khukhúše, khuwá, khíza, khéya, khí, khuté

Khukh**ú**še waŋ **kh**úža š**kh**é.

K ská, ká, kóze, kíze, kiŋ, kú, kúŋ, kéye

Ká **k**imímela s**k**á **k**iŋ **k**ú.

3 🔊 Hold out your hand and try the first word.
Do you feel the puff of air on your hand?

4 🔊 Now, try the second word, but try to say it without the puff of air.

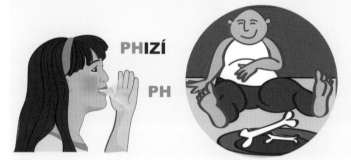

PHIZÍ

PH

PÍZE

P

PH phí, philámayaye, phizí, iphíyake, wóphila, íphi

Yu**ph**í**ph**iya wí**ph**i čha iyók**ph**i.

P spáya, pahá, pemní, pi, píza, pispíza, po, púza

Pis**p**íza í**p**uza**p**i eyá **p**ablú**p**i.

5 🔊 Hold out your hand and try the first word.
Do you feel the puff of air on your hand?

6 🔊 Now, try the second word, but try to say it without the puff of air.

THEZÍ

TH

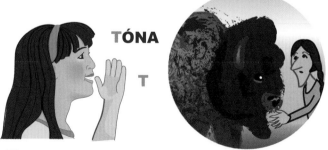

TÓNA

T

TH thí, thípi, thiyópa, thiyóle, čhethí, éthi, theȟíla,

Thibló é**th**i na čhe**th**í.

T stáka, táku, ité, tóna, tuwá, tuktél

Ik**t**ó o**t**ú**t**uya p**t**é wa**š**té waŋ yus**t**ós**t**o.

Review Quiz

1 What do you know how to do? Match the questions with the correct picture, and then write an answer, like the example:

Háŋ, lowáŋpi uŋmáspe /
Hiyá, lowáŋpi uŋmáspe šni.

1. Wakhúl yápi uŋníspe he?

2. Wakšúpi uŋníspe he?

3. Šuŋk'ákaŋyaŋkapi uŋníspe he?

4. Čhethípi uŋníspe he?

5. Wičhítowapi uŋníspe he?

6. Síthapa škátapi uŋníspe he?

7. Thabškátapi uŋníspe he?

8. Wačhípi uŋníspe he?

2 For each of these answers, can you write the question, like the example?

Háŋ, wanúŋwe --> Yanúŋwaŋ he?

1. Háŋ, walówaŋ.

_____

2. Hiyá, čhaŋwákabu šni.

_____

3. Háŋ, wawáčhi.

_____

4. Háŋ, wówapi blawá.

_____

5. Hiyá, wawákšu šni.

_____

6. Háŋ waíŋmnaŋke.

_____

7. Háŋ, thabwáškate.

_____

8. Hiyá, šuŋk'ákaŋmaŋke šni.

_____

3 a What do you like to do? Can you answer these questions about your activities, like the example:

Háŋ, lowáŋ awáštewalake. /
Hiyá, lowáŋ awáštewalake šni.

1. Thabškál awášteyalaka he?
2. Wakhúl yá awášteyalaka he?
3. Nuŋwáŋ awášteyalaka he?
4. Wakšú awášteyalaka he?
5. Šuŋk'ákaŋyaŋg awášteyalaka he?

b Next, ask your partner whether he or she likes these activities, and write sentences about him or her on scrap paper, like the example:

[čhažé] lowáŋ awáštelake. /
[čhažé] lowáŋ awáštelake šni.

4 Here are some questions the children are writing for interviews. Can you tell if they are asking one person, or more than one person? Put a check in the correct column for each question.

	one person	more than one person
1. Wayáčhipi he?		
2. Wayáčhi he?		
3. Yalówaŋpi he?		
4. Yalówaŋ he?		
5. Yanúŋwaŋpi he?		
6. Yanúŋwaŋ he?		

5 You are interviewing the people for a newspaper article for your school. For each activity, write a question to the people in the picture. Remember, you need to think, each time, about whether you are talking to one person, or more than one person.

thabškátA   wakšú

íŋyaŋkA   wówapi yawá

šuŋk'ákaŋyaŋkA   čhaŋkábu

1 🔊 **a** Bob is asking his friends where they are going for the weekend. First, listen and fill in the person each child is visiting.

b Then, listen again and fill in the speech bubbles with the missing words at the end of the sentences.

_____ thí kiŋ ektá mníŋ _____.

Tókhiya níŋ kta he?

_Uŋčí___ thí kiŋ ektá mníŋ kte.

_____ thí kiŋ ektá _____ ___.

_____ thí kiŋ ektá mníŋ kte.

_____ thí kiŋ ektá _____ ___.

_____ thí kiŋ ektá mníŋ _____.

_____ thí kiŋ _____ _____ ___.

2 **a** Now write about yourself: Where will you go this weekend? Write 2-3 sentences about where you will go, like the children said above.

b Find out where everyone is going! Ask three of your classmates where they will go this weekend. Mark their answers in the chart.

_____

_____

_____

_____

Čhažé	"Tókhiya níŋ kta he?"

č Take out a piece of scrap paper and write what you found out about your classmates, like the model:
Summer Lisa thí kiŋ ektá yíŋ kte.

3 You're in a new town. Do you recognize these buildings? Fill in the missing building names! If you don't remember the words, check in your dictionary.

owóškate

wíčhitenašķanškaŋ othí

wówapi othí

mázaska thípi

Mike thí kiŋ

4 Imagine where the groups of children will go based on the map above. Choose one group and write several sentences about where they will go on scrap paper.. With a partner, correct each other's sentences.

5 Work with a partner. Each of you will choose one of the groups of children (in the top right corner of the map). Choose a destination for each child in your group, and draw a line from the child to the place that that they will go.

Then, ask questions about where your partner's children will go, like in the example:

> **Lisa tókhiya yíŋ kta he?**

> **Lisa owóte thípi-ta yíŋ kte.**

6 You're going to turn your classroom into a town! Your teacher will label different parts of the room with different place names. Then, the whole class will stand at the board, and start the game.

Your teacher will ask you where you will go. Tell him/her where you will go, and go there, like in the example:

> **David, tókhiya níŋ kta he?**

> **Owóte thípi-ta mníŋ kte.**

73

Wóuŋspe 6

7 **a** The children are inviting each other to go somewhere. Where will they go? Who will they go with? Listen and match the pair with their destination.

b Now, listen again. Listen to the response and see if the other character agrees to go or not. Put a check next to each pair that is actually going to go to the place.

Lisa: Ťhašína, wačhípi-ta uŋyáŋ héči?
Ťhašína: Háŋ, uŋyíŋ kte.

owáyazaŋ othí

wačhípi ✓

owóte thípi

wígli oínažiŋ

mas'óphiye

oíčhimani thípi

oyúžužu thípi

owáčhekiye

wówapi othí

owáyawa

mázaská thípi

wičhítenaškaŋškaŋ othí

phéta oínažiŋ

wakpá

8 Think of three places you would like to go this weekend. Now, how would you invite a friend to go with you to each of those places? Write down what you would say, like the example.

Rapid City-ta uŋyáŋ héči?

Next, ask three different people if they will go there too. Have three separate conversations. Who will go with you?

Rapid City-ta uŋyáŋ héči?

Háŋ, uŋyíŋ kte.

9 Lisa and Ťhašína will go to the powwow together. Where will the other pairs of children go? The teacher is writing text messages to let all the parents know. Can you help him? On a piece of scrap paper, write a sentence about each pair. Follow the model below.

Lisa Ťhašína kičhí wačhípi-ta yápi kte.

10 Abléza po!

Look at the sentence to the right. Which word do we add to show that Lisa and Tȟašína are going together? Circle it!

> **Lisa Tȟašína kičhí wačhípi-ta yápi kte.**

11 These children also have a busy weekend! Can you figure out where each pair of children will go? Write a sentence about each pair, like the example.

1 *James Summer kičhí owóškate—ta yápi kte.*

2 _____

3 _____

4 _____

12 Now's it's Saturday, and Lisa's Mom has been making lunch for Lisa and all of her friends! But when she calls them, she realizes that they have all left for somewhere already. Lisa's little sister is telling her Mom where all of the children have left for. Can you finish Lisa's sister's sentences, like the model?

> James Summer kičhí tókhi iyáyapi he?

> *James Summer kičhí owáškate—ta iyáyapi.*

> Lisa Kimi kičhí tókhi iyáyapi he?

> _____

> Bob Tȟašína kičhí tókhi iyáyapi he?

> _____

> Mike Matȟó kičhí tókhi iyáyapi he?

> _____

13 Abléza po!

Look at the examples to the right and answer the questions below.

1. In the first picture Mathó is answering Summer's invitation. What verb form does he use? Write it here: _____

2. In the second picture Mathó is telling his dad what he and Summer will do. What verb form does he use?
   Write it here: _____

> Mathó, thaŋkál uŋyíŋ kta he?
>
> Ohaŋ, thaŋkál uŋyíŋ kte.
>
> Até, Summer kičhí thaŋkál uŋyáŋpi kte.

14 Take a card from your teacher and invite a friend to come with you for the activity on the card. Will they go with you or not? Report to the teacher, like in the example.

> Owóte thípi-ta uŋyíŋ kta he?
>
> Háŋ, uŋyíŋ kte.

> Owóte thípi-ta uŋyáŋpi kte.
>
> Ohaŋ, yá pe.

15 🔊 First, look at what each of the characters is holding, and guess where he or she **is going**. Draw a line to match the person with the place. Then, listen and see if your guess is correct.

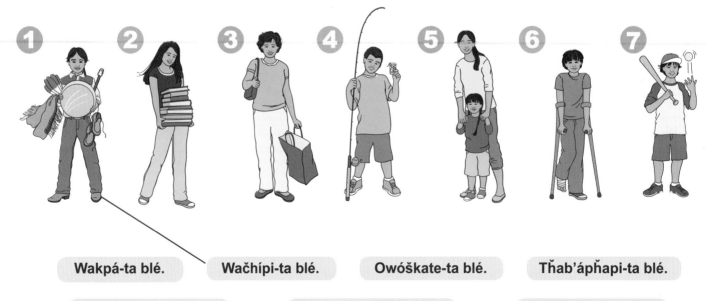

① ② ③ ④ ⑤ ⑥ ⑦

Wakpá-ta blé.	Wačhípi-ta blé.	Owóškate-ta blé.	Thab'áphapi-ta blé.
Mas'óphiye-ta blé.	Owáyazaŋ othí-ta blé.	Wówapi othí-ta blé.	

16 Your partner will pretend to be one of the people below. Try to guess who he/she is! Ask questions about where he or she is going, like the models.

Owáyazaŋ othí-ta lá he?

Háŋ, owáyazaŋ othí-ta blé!

Oháŋ, čha Jason niyé!

Jason

Karen

Maťhó

Bob

Mike

Connie
Alexa kičhí

Patty

17 ⓐ Choose your favorite three characters from the previous activity and write a sentence about each of them, like the example.

Jason owáyazaŋ othí-ta yé.

ⓑ Read the sentences you wrote to your partner and your partner will point to who you're talking about.

18 Look again at the map on pg 73. Pretend that you are going to one of those places. When your classmates ask you, tell them where you **are going.**

Ask one or two of your classmates where they **are going** and take notes, like in the model.

Tókhiya lá he?

(place)-ta blé.

David (place)-ta yé.

iyáye

í

19 Look how Kimi recorded the time that Bob left the starting point. Can you finish the sentences for the other children's times? Use the model.

Bob 3:40 k'uŋ héhaŋ iyáye.

Mike 3:53

James 3:40

Matȟó 3:29

Lisa 3:39

Summer 3:45

Tȟašína 3:51

20 Bob got to the tree at 3:55. Working with a partner, say the time that one of the children got to the tree - your partner will say which child you're thinking of.

Bob: 3:55
Mike: 4:00
James: 3:50
Matȟó: 3:50
Lisa: 3:50
Summer: 4:10
Tȟašína: 4:00

Tuwá 3:55 k'uŋ héhaŋ í?

Bob 3:55 k'uŋ héhaŋ í!

21 Kimi needs help doing the math! You know what time each child left the starting line, and what time they got to the tree - can you figure out how long each child was on his or her way?

You can use a piece of scrap paper to count. When you have the answers, write final results here. Write them in order of slowest runner to the fastest. Write the fastest in Kimi's speech bubble, so that Kimi can announce the winner!

Bob oȟ'áŋkȟo akézaptaŋ hehányaŋ yé.

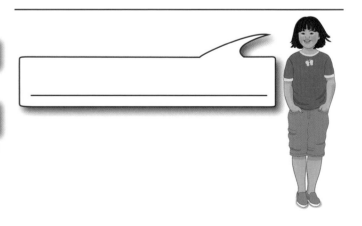

22 Now, it's Monday morning. The kids are talking about where they went. Listen and circle the children who went where they said they would go.

- **Lisa, nikȟúŋši thí kiŋ ektá yaí he?**
- **Háŋ, waí.**

23 Using the information from the previous activity, write an email to say where Lisa and all the other children went.

Iyáyeya   Iȟpéya   Égnaka

From:

To:

Subject:

Lisa kȟúŋšitku thí kiŋ ektá i.

24 Interview two classmates about where they went for the weekend. Put a check next to the places on the survey that they went.

a		1	2
1.	Owóte thípi-ta yaí he?		
2.	Owóškate-ta yaí he?		
3.	Mas'óphiye-ta yaí he?		
4.	Owáčhekiye-ta yaí he?		
5.	Owáyazaŋ othí-ta yaí he?		
6.	Wówapi othí-ta yaí he?		
7.	Wičhítenaškaŋškaŋ othí-ta yaí he?		
8.	Wakpá-ta yaí he?		

b		1	2
1.	Nikȟúŋši thí kiŋ ektá yaí he?		
2.	Nitȟúŋkašila thí kiŋ ektá yaí he?		
3.	Nitȟúŋwiŋ thí kiŋ ektá yaí he?		
4.	Nilékši thí kiŋ ektá yaí he?		
5.	Nitȟáŋhaŋši / Ničépȟaŋši / Nišíč'eši / Niháŋkaši thí kiŋ ektá yaí he?		
6.	Ničhíye/Nithíblo thí kiŋ ektá yaí he?		
7.	Nitȟáŋke/Ničhúwe thí kiŋ ektá yaí he?		

25 Write a few sentences about where your classmates went, like in the example. When you're finished, compare your writing with a partner.

Peter David thí kiŋ ektá i.
Peter tȟuŋwíŋču thí kiŋ ektá i.

26 Matȟó's mother is very angry at him! Here's his side of the story - can you figure out why his mother might be upset? First, skim through the story and find out how much money Matȟó has when he gets home. Write the amount here: _____

Híŋhaŋni iná heyé, "Čhiŋkší, mas'óphiye-ta yá ye," eyé. Ho čha, hepȟé, "Ohán, táku čha opȟéwathuŋ kta he?" epȟé. Yuŋkȟáŋ iná heyé, "Bló etáŋ é na wagmúšpaŋšni waŋží é na wagmíza etáŋ opȟétȟuŋ we," eyé. Ho čha Mike thí kiŋ ečhétkiya ibláble. Mníŋ na waí, éyaš Mike él yaŋké šni. Ho čha akhé mníŋ na wígli oínažiŋ kiŋ ektá waí. Héčhiya čhaŋmháŋska waštéšte eyá opȟéwathuŋ. Yuŋkȟáŋ Summer waŋblákiŋ na čhaŋmháŋska waŋ wak'ú. Summer heyé, "Tókhiya lá he?" eyá imáyuŋǧe. Ho čha hepȟé "Mas'óphiye-ta blé," epȟé. Na heháŋl hepȟé: "Uŋyáŋ héči?" epȟá yuŋkȟáŋ íŋš heyé, "Hiyá, uŋyíŋ kte šni, ičhíŋ omákȟaŋ šni," eyé.

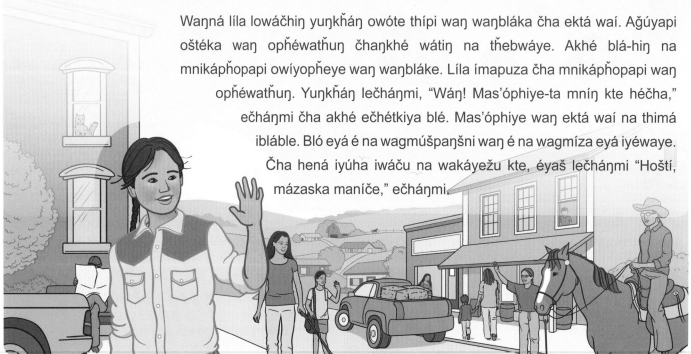

Waŋná líla lowáčhiŋ yuŋkȟáŋ owóte thípi waŋ waŋbláka čha ektá waí. Aǧúyapi oštéka waŋ opȟéwathuŋ čhaŋkhé wátiŋ na tȟebwáye. Akhé blá-hiŋ na mnikápȟopapi owíyopȟeye waŋ waŋbláke. Líla ímapuza čha mnikápȟopapi waŋ opȟéwathuŋ. Yuŋkȟáŋ lečháŋmi, "Wáŋ! Mas'óphiye-ta mníŋ kte héčha," ečháŋmi čha akhé ečhétkiya blé. Mas'óphiye waŋ ektá waí na thimá ibláble. Bló eyá é na wagmúšpaŋšni waŋ é na wagmíza eyá iyéwaye. Čha hená iyúha iwáču na wakáyežu kte, éyaš lečháŋmi "Hoští, mázaska maníče," ečháŋmi.

27 **ⓐ** Number the places in the order that Matȟó visits them.

____ Mike thí kiŋ
____ Mas'óphiye
____ Owóte thípi waŋ
____ Wígli oínažiŋ waŋ

ⓑ **Matȟó húŋku kiŋ táku čhíŋ he? Wičhóiye kiŋ ókšaŋkšaŋ kazó wo.**

28 Read the story again and answer these questions. Write your answers on a piece of scrap paper.

A) Matȟó tȟokéya tókhiya yá he?
B) Mike thiyáta yaŋká he?
Č) Na heháŋl tókhiya yá he?
E) Wígli oínažiŋ kiŋ ektá Matȟó táku opȟétȟuŋ he?
G) Matȟó Summer táku k'ú he?
Ǧ) Matȟó táku yúta he?
H) Húŋku kiŋ táku čhíŋ kiŋ hená Matȟó opȟétȟuŋ kta he?

29

No one was home during the weekend! Bob is asking his friend whom they went to visit during the weekend. Listen and match the characters with where they went.

lekšítku thí kiŋ

kȟúŋšitku thí kiŋ

tȟuŋkášitku thí kiŋ

čhiyéku thí kiŋ

tȟaŋháŋšitku thí kiŋ

tȟuŋwíŋču thí kiŋ

čépȟaŋšitku thí kiŋ

thiblóku thí kiŋ

čhuwéku thí kiŋ

30

Lisa's mom is giving Lisa some directions. Can you figure out where she wants Lisa to go? Listen and follow along with the directions. Draw an X on the place where Lisa is supposed to meet her mom later on and write it into the instructions.

1. Mázaská thípi kiŋ hetáŋhaŋ iyáya yo/ye.
2. Tȟoká, owótȟaŋla yá yo/ye.
3. Heháŋl, čhatkáyatakiya yá yo/ye.
4. Owáyawa kiŋ iyópteya yá yo/ye.
5. Išláyatakiya yá yo/ye.
6. Ehákeȟčiŋ _____ kiŋ wówapi othí kiŋ isákhib hé.

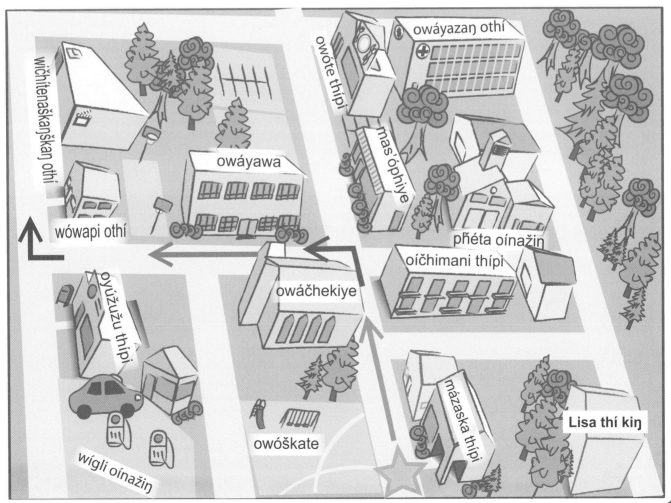

31 Let's take a walk around our "town"! Label places in your classroom like places in a town.

Your teacher will give you directions on where to go around the classroom. Can you guess where the teacher is leading you?

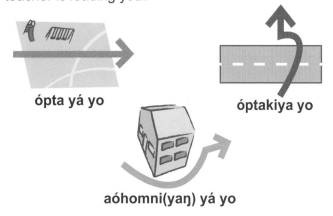

ópta yá yo

óptakiya yo

aóhomni(yaŋ) yá yo

32 Lisa wants to get some snacks at the gas station to take to the movies, but she doesn't know how to get there from her house. Can you help draw a map for her? Follow the directions below and draw the path onto the map.

1) **Tȟoká čhatkáyatakiya yá yo.**

2) **Oíčhimani thípi kiŋ iyópteya yá yo.**

3) **Akhé čhatkáyatakiya yá yo.**

4) **Owóškate kiŋ ópta yá yo.**

5) **Čhaŋkú kiŋ óptakiya yo.**

33 Okay, now it's your turn! Pick a spot where your partner is supposed to meet you. On a piece of scrap paper, write directions for him/her to get there. Next, say the directions out loud to your partner. Can he/she draw the route you said on the map?

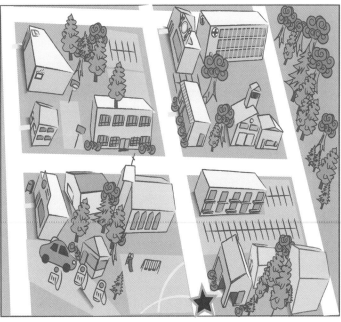

34 a Now, take out a piece of scrap paper and draw a map of your town, or part of your town. Label the streets and buildings, and your house.

b Next, on a piece of scratch paper, write directions for how to get from a place in town to your house.

č Then, give your map to your partner. Tell your partner the directions you wrote. Can he/she draw the route on the map?

Review Quiz

1 Can you fill in the missing words in the children's conversations? See if you can do this without looking back in the chapter.

1. Lisa: Tókhiya _____ kta he?

    Summer: _____ ektá _____ kte. Ógle ťhéča waŋží opȟéwatȟuŋ kte ȟčiŋ.

2. Mike: Lisa _____ _____ kta he?

    James: Lisa _____ _____ ektá _____ kte. Wówapi waŋží yawá kte.

3. Matȟó: James Mike kičhí _____ _____ _____ he?

    Bob: James Mike kičhí _____ _____ ektá _____ kte. Šuŋk'ákaŋyaŋkapi kte.

4. Ťȟašína: Kimi, _____ _____ -ta _____ héči? Líla lowáčhiŋ!

    Kimi: Háŋ, _____ kte.

2 Some of the children are planning to go various places, but they don't want to go alone! How would they ask someone to go with them? Can you fill in the speech bubble for each child according to the place (in parentheses) he/she wants to go?

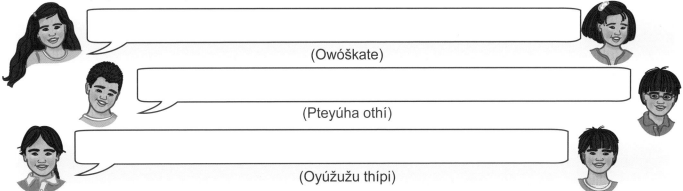

(Owóškate)

(Pteyúha othí)

(Oyúžužu thípi)

3 Now, can you write about where the two children are going, from the speech bubbles above? Write on scrap paper, like the example: *James Mike kičhí pteyúha othí-ta yápi kte.*

4 Challenge: How would you say the following sentences in Lakota?

1. Where will you go tomorrow?

2. Tomorrow I will go to the hospital.

3. Where did they go yesterday?

4. I am on my way to the library now.

5. Ťȟašína, let's go to the playground!

6. Last summer, I went to Rapid City.

7. Mom, Bob and I will go to the movie theater.

8. Dad, Bob and Lisa are on their way to the post office now.

5 It's Friday evening, and the children have all left for different places for the weekend! Where have they left for? Can you write some text messages to let everyone know? Use the clues to help you write your sentences. Write on scrap paper.

Lisa	-->	Wazí Aháŋhaŋ
Bob	-->	Mnilúzahe Othúŋwahe
Mike	-->	Waŋblí Pahá
Ťȟašína	-->	Ȟeská Othúŋwahe
Kimi	-->	Matȟó Akíčhita
Matȟó	-->	Íŋyaŋša Oók'e

Lisa: Wazí Aháŋhaŋ-ta iyáye.

1 Where did Lisa invite these people to go? Listen and match the place with the friend she invited to that place.

owóte-thípi   wówapi othí   wígli oínažiŋ   wakpá

wačhípi   mas'óphiye   šuŋk'ónažiŋ

2 Listen again. Who agreed to go with her? Circle their names.

James   Tȟašína   Bob   Kimi   Matȟó   Summer   Mike

3 Which word did Lisa use when she said "I want to go with you"? Underline it.

Mníŋ kte.   Uŋyáŋpi kte.   Uŋyíŋ kte.   Yápi kte.

4 The teacher will label places around the room. Sit in a circle with the whole class. Choose one classmate to invite to go with you to one of the places in the room. Invite them as in the model:

Michael, Waŋblí Pahá-ta uŋyíŋ kta he?

Oháŋ, uŋyíŋ kte. / Hiyá, uŋyíŋ kte šni.

Mnilúzahe   Otȟúnwahe

Waŋblí Pahá

84

Bob: Waŋná maǧážu k'uŋ hé akísni.
Čha Mike thí kiŋ ektá uŋyíŋ kta he?

Lisa: Hiyá, uŋyíŋ kte šni.

Bob: Ho čha wičhítenaškaŋškaŋ waŋyáŋg
uŋyáŋkiŋ kta he?

Lisa: Hiyá, waŋyáŋg uŋyáŋkiŋ kte šni.

Bob: Lowáŋpi etáŋ anáuŋǧoptaŋ kta he?

Lisa: Hiyá, anáuŋǧoptaŋ kte šni.

Bob: Pizza Hut ektá waúŋyutiŋ kta he?

Lisa: Hiyá, waúŋyutiŋ kte šni, lowáčhiŋ šni.

Bob: Wóuŋspe omnáye kiŋ uŋ uŋškátiŋ kta he?

Lisa: Hiyá, uŋškátiŋ kte šni.

Bob: Ho čha tȟaŋkál uŋyíŋ kta he?

Lisa: Oháŋ, uŋyíŋ kte.

Bob: Até, Lisa kičhí tȟaŋkál uŋyáŋpi kte ló.

5 Match the picture with the part of the text where Bob and Lisa are talking about the activity. Draw a line, like in the model.

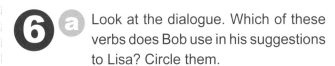

6 **a** Look at the dialogue. Which of these verbs does Bob use in his suggestions to Lisa? Circle them.

yÁ	wačhí
anáǧoptaŋ	wakšú
íŋyaŋkA	škátA
nuŋwÁŋ	wótA
šuŋk'ákaŋyaŋkA	waŋyáŋg yaŋkÁ

b Read the dialogue again, and answer the questions about Bob and Lisa's discussion.

1. Waŋná maǧážu he?   Háŋ / Hiyá
2. Mike thí kiŋ ektá yápi kta he?   Háŋ / Hiyá
3. Wičhítenaškaŋškaŋ waŋyáŋg   Háŋ / Hiyá
   yaŋkápi kta he?
4. Lowáŋpi etáŋ anáǧoptaŋpi kta he?   Háŋ / Hiyá
5. Pizza Hut ektá wótapi kta he?   Háŋ / Hiyá
6. Lisa ločhíŋ he?   Háŋ / Hiyá
7. Wóuŋspe omnáye kiŋ uŋ škátapi kta   Háŋ / Hiyá
   he?
8. Tȟáŋkal yápi kta he?   Háŋ / Hiyá

7 Abléza po!

- We call syllables like **-uŋ**- a **personal affix**. What other personal affixes do you see in the words below?
- Where do you add **-uŋ**- to a word? Look at these examples, and then add the missing **-uŋ**- to the words below.

walówaŋ	nawážiŋ	iyómakiphi
uŋlówaŋ	naúŋžiŋ	iyóuŋkiphi

1s: **walówaŋ**　　　1s: **mawáni**
1d: uŋlówan　　　　1d:

1s: **waškáte**　　　1s: **wanúŋwe**
1d:　　　　　　　　1d:

- On these words you add the **-uŋ**- in the same place as you add what other forms? ("I" form? "you" form? "they" form?)
Write them here: _____

8

First, on a piece of scratch paper, make a list of the dictionary forms for each of the verbs below.

~~uŋlówaŋ~~, naúŋžiŋ, iyóuŋkiphi, maúŋni, uŋkóle, uŋk'íŋyaŋke, slol'úŋye

The "you and I" personal affix is attached to verbs in different ways, depending on the verb. Can you write each of the verbs above in the correct box, depending on the way the affix is attached, like the model?

uŋ
　uŋlówan

uŋk

uŋk'

'uŋ(k)

9 Abléza po!

a

What about the words below? Is **-uŋ/ uŋk/'uŋk/uŋk'**- always in the same place as the "I" affixes (1s), like **wa** and **bl**?

íblotake	owále	waíŋmnaŋke
uŋkíyotake	uŋkóle	uŋk'íŋyaŋke

b

Now, look up the words below in the New Lakota Dictionary. Scan through the entry and look for the "I" form (1s:) and the "you and I" form (1p: without **-pi** ending), and write them here, like in the model:

olé　　　　　　　**uŋspé**
1s: owále　　　　　1s:
1d: uŋkóle　　　　　1d:

slolyÁ　　　　　**úŋ**
1s:　　　　　　　　1s:
1d:　　　　　　　　1d:

10

Help Lisa out! Lisa's cousin is coming to visit. She wants to suggest some activities for them to do together on the weekend. Can you write the sentences she would use? You can use the verbs below.

škátA
nuŋwÁŋ
owóte-ta yÁ
íŋyaŋkA
wačhí
wakšú
íyotakA
wótA

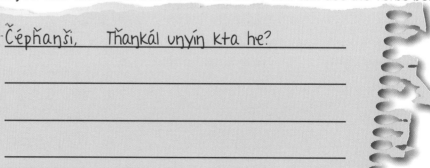

Čépȟaŋši,　Tȟaŋkál uŋyíŋ kta he?

11 Let's review inviting and reporting!
Look at the examples to the right and answer the questions.

A) In the first picture Matȟó is answering Summer's invitation. What verb form does he use? Write it here: _____

B) In the second picture Matȟó is telling his dad what he and Summer will do. What verb form does he use? Write it here: _____

Matȟó, tȟaŋkál uŋškátiŋ kte?

Oháŋ, uŋškátiŋ kte.

Até, Summer kičhí uŋškátapi kte.

12 In these pictures, are the children inviting or reporting? Fill in the blanks with the correct form of one of the verbs from the list.

Hoúŋkhuwa kte.　Uŋnúŋwiŋ kte.　Waúŋkšu kte.　Waúŋchi kte.
Hoúŋkhuwapi kte.　Uŋnúŋwaŋpi kte.　Waúŋkšupi kte.　Waúŋchipi kte.

13 First, invite your partner to do three activities with you. Have three different conversations! You can use the verbs that Lisa used in activity 10!

Then, on a piece of scratch paper, or on the board, write sentences to report what you are doing with a classmate, like the model.

Uŋnúŋwiŋ kta he?

Háŋ, uŋnúŋwiŋ kte. / Hiyá, uŋnúŋwiŋ kte šni.

14 Being able to talk about plant names and parts is an important part of Lakota culture. Why? For the Lakota people, green things that grow from Grandmother Earth, like trees and plants, are sacred. Matȟó admires his grandmother because she has the traditional Lakota knowledge of plants and trees.

He wants to learn all this himself, so he is working on a webpage about trees in Lakota.

Can you finish labeling this drawing of trees for Matȟó? Some of the words you may know, others, you may have to check in the dictionary.

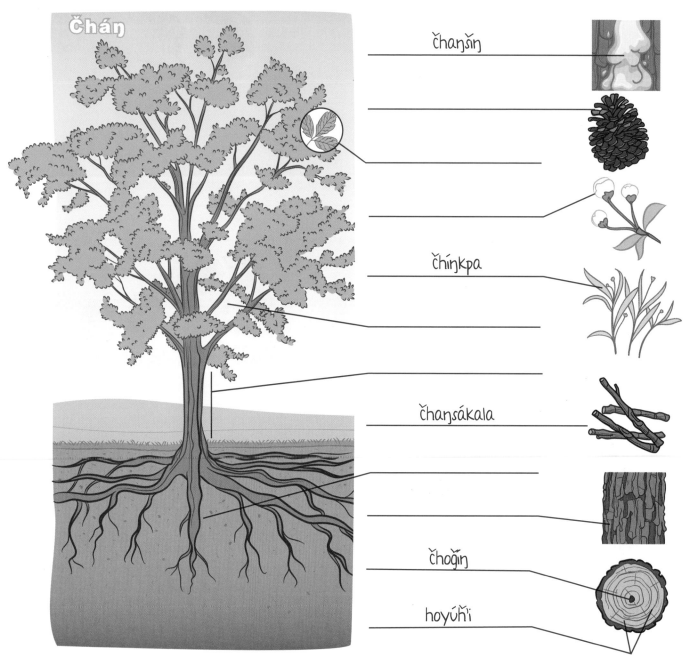

Čháŋ

čhaŋšiŋ

čhíŋkpa

čhaŋsákala

čhoǧíŋ

hoyúȟ'i

15 Build the tree! Your teacher will give you a card with a word on it naming a part of the tree. You will be building the tree in the center of the room with your classmates. When you hear the word called, go and stand at the right spot for the word you have! The roots, for example, should not stand at the top of the tree! When the teacher calls your word, go and stand in the right place.

16 **a** Like Lisa and Bob, Matȟó really likes being outside! But, he's also good with computers. Right now, he is making a web page with information about the plants and trees that grow in Lakota country. Which trees do you know? Circle them.

b Now, skim the guide. What kinds of information does Matȟó give us about the trees? Circle all the correct choices. **color / age / height / leaf shape / roots / changes in winter**

Čháŋ kiŋ lená Lakȟóta makȟóčhe kiŋ imáhel ičháǧe.
Na Lakȟóta kiŋ čháŋ kiŋ lená ilágyapi.

Pséȟtiŋ
- Čhaŋhá kiŋ ȟóta.
- Waníyetu čháŋna čhaŋwápe waníče.
- Čháŋ kiŋ lé líla háŋske.
- Čhaŋwápe kiŋ tȟotȟó.

Wazíčhaŋ
- Čhaŋhá kiŋ ǧí.
- Čháŋ kiŋ lé háŋske.
- Waníyetu čháŋna čhaŋwápe ikȟóyake.
- Čhaŋwápe kiŋ zibzípela.

Ȟaŋté
- Čhaŋhá kiŋ ǧí.
- Čháŋ kiŋ lé ptéčela.
- Waníyetu čháŋna čhaŋwápe ikȟóyake.
- Watȟókeča kiŋ gmigmégmela.
- Watȟókeča kiŋ tȟotȟó.

Čhaŋšáša
- Čhaŋhá kiŋ šá.
- Wanáȟča skaská ikȟóyake.
- Čhaŋwápe kiŋ háŋskaska.
- Waníyetu čháŋna čhaŋwápe waníče.
- Čhaŋȟáka kiŋ lé ptéčela/hukȟúčiyela.

17 Matȟó is having trouble finishing some of the descriptions! Can you help him find the missing information? Look at the pictures of the leaves and write in the correct leaf description for each tree. Choose from the descriptions below:

- ~~Čhaŋwápe kiŋ pȟestóstola.~~
- Čhaŋwápe kiŋ háŋskaska.

- Čhaŋwápe kiŋ oíse-yámni.
- Čhaŋwápe kiŋ čikčík'ala.

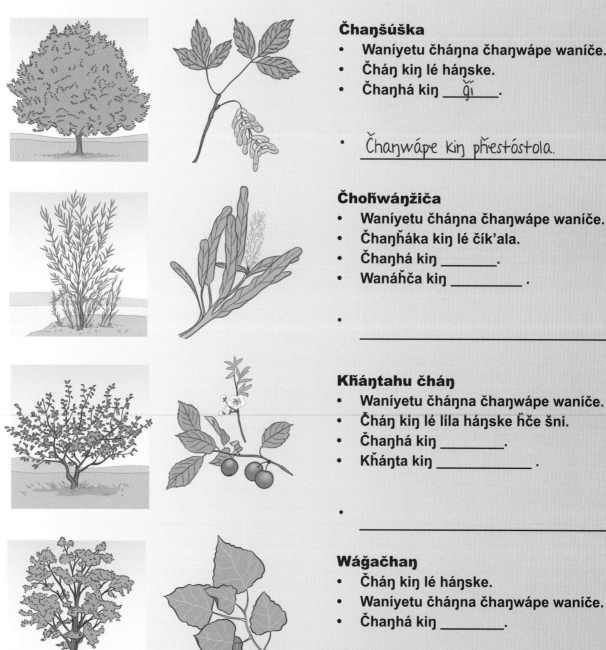

Čhaŋšúŝka
- Waníyetu čháŋna čhaŋwápe waníče.
- Čháŋ kiŋ lé háŋske.
- Čhaŋhá kiŋ ___ǧí___ .

- Čhaŋwápe kiŋ pȟestóstola.

Čhoȟwáŋžiča
- Waníyetu čháŋna čhaŋwápe waníče.
- Čhaŋȟáka kiŋ lé čík'ala.
- Čhaŋhá kiŋ _____ .
- Wanáȟča kiŋ _____ .

- _____

Kȟáŋtahu čháŋ
- Waníyetu čháŋna čhaŋwápe waníče.
- Čháŋ kiŋ lé líla háŋske ȟče šni.
- Čhaŋhá kiŋ _____ .
- Kȟáŋta kiŋ _____ .

- _____

Wáǧačhaŋ
- Čháŋ kiŋ lé háŋske.
- Waníyetu čháŋna čhaŋwápe waníče.
- Čhaŋhá kiŋ _____ .

- _____

18 Abléza po!

a Look at the pairs of sentences about trees. Which ones are plural? Put a check mark next to the plural sentences.

Čaŋwápe kiŋ lé tȟó.
Čaŋwápe kiŋ lená tȟotȟó.

Čháŋ kiŋ lé háŋske.
Čháŋ kiŋ lená háŋskaska.

Wazíphiŋkpa kiŋ lé ǧí.
Wazíphiŋkpa kiŋ lená ǧiǧí.

Watȟókeča kiŋ lé gmigméla.
Watȟókeča kiŋ lená gmigmégmela.

Čaŋwápe kiŋ lé tȟáŋka.
Čaŋwápe kiŋ lená tȟaŋkíŋkiŋyaŋ.

b What is different about the word **tȟó** in the sentence that talks about more than one thing?
What changes are there in the other verbs? Can you write them on scratch paper?
We call this change **reduplication.**

19 Here are some more verbs! Look up their reduplicated forms in the dictionary and write them below.

šá	_____	ptéčela	_____
tȟó	_____	sápa	_____
háŋska	_____	pȟéstola	_____

20 Can you write sentences about the objects in the pictures? Write one sentence for each picture, describing the objects, like the examples above. Here are some words to choose from:

ská/skaská, háŋske/háŋskaska, tȟáŋka/tȟaŋkíŋkiŋyaŋ, čík'ala/
čikčík'ala, kȟáte/kȟalkȟáte, pȟé/pȟepȟé, šóke/šokšóke

Wanáȟča kiŋ lé _____ .

Wanáȟča kiŋ lená _____ .

Ikȟáŋ kiŋ lé _____ .

Ikȟáŋ kiŋ lená _____ .

Tȟápa kiŋ lé_____.

Tȟápa kiŋ lená _____.

Pȟešníža kiŋ lé _____ .

Pȟešníža kiŋ lená _____ .

Tȟápa kiŋ lé _____.

Tȟápa kiŋ lená _____.

Míla kiŋ lé _____ .

Míla kiŋ lená _____.

Šiná kiŋ lé _____ .

Šiná kiŋ lená _____ .

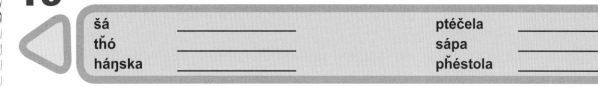

21 Why not start your own tree scrapbook in Lakota? Find a leaf and glue it or draw it on your own scrapbook page below. Then, write a short description of that tree, like the models below.

Čháŋ kiŋ lé tȟáŋka / čik'ala.
Čhaŋwápe kiŋ lená tȟaŋkíŋkiŋyaŋ / čikčik'ala.

_____

_____

_____

_____

22 Listen to Bob describing a tree from his scrapbook, and on a piece of scrap paper, draw the picture as he describes it. What kind of tree have you drawn? Look at the tree guides 1 and 2 and find the name!

Write it here: _____

23 Let's play a matching game! Each sentence on the left is the opposite of one of the sentences on the right! Match up all the pairs of opposites by drawing a line, like the example.

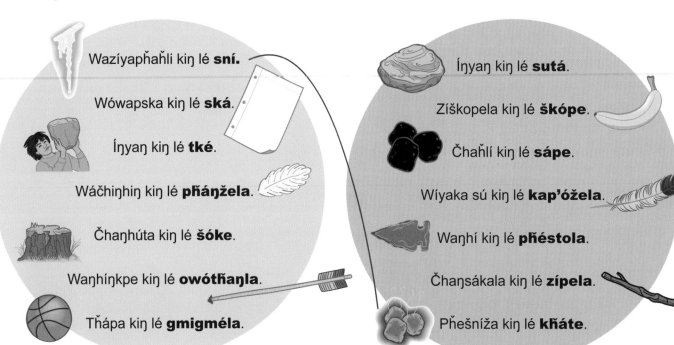

Wazíyapȟaȟli kiŋ lé **sní.**

Wówapska kiŋ lé **ská.**

Íŋyaŋ kiŋ lé **tké.**

Wáčhiŋhiŋ kiŋ lé **pȟáŋžela.**

Čhaŋhúta kiŋ lé **šóke.**

Waŋhíŋkpe kiŋ lé **owótȟaŋla.**

Tȟápa kiŋ lé **gmigméla.**

Íŋyaŋ kiŋ lé **sutá.**

Zíškopela kiŋ lé **škópe.**

Čhaȟlí kiŋ lé **sápe.**

Wíyaka sú kiŋ lé **kap'óžela.**

Waŋhí kiŋ lé **pȟéstola.**

Čhaŋsákala kiŋ lé **zípela.**

Pȟešníža kiŋ lé **kȟáte.**

24 Tȟašína is trying to write sentences that talk about more than one of each object. Can you help her? Find the correct reduplicated form for each sentence from the list, and finish writing the sentence.

snisní, skaská, tketké, pȟaŋšpȟáŋžela, šokšóke, owótȟaŋtȟaŋla, gmigmégmela, kȟalkȟáte, sapsápe, kap'óšp'ožela, suksúta, zibzípela, škoškópe, pȟestóstola

1. Wazíyapȟaȟli kiŋ lená _____ .

2. Wówapska kiŋ lená _____ .

3. Íŋyaŋ kiŋ lená _____ .

4. Wáčhiŋhiŋ kiŋ lená _____ .

5. Čhaŋhúta kiŋ lená _____ .

6. Waŋhíŋkpe kiŋ lená _____ .

7. Tȟápa kiŋ lená _____ .

8. Pȟešníža kiŋ lená _____ .

9. Čhaȟlí kiŋ lená _____ .

10. Wáǧačhaŋ sú kiŋ lená _____ .

11. Íŋyaŋ kiŋ lená _____ .

12. Čhaŋsákala kiŋ lená _____ .

13. Zíškopela kiŋ lená _____ .

14. Waŋhí kiŋ lená _____ .

25 **a** Work with a partner. Think of an object, and say what it is like. Your partner should guess what object you are thinking of, like this:

Táku kiŋ lé tké.

Lé íŋyaŋ héčha.

b Now let's talk about more than one of the same object! Describe them and your partner will guess, like in the example:

Táku kiŋ lená tketké.

Lená íŋyaŋ héčha.

26 a

Let's look at the traditional uses of different trees! Write the name of the tree under the picture of its use. Be careful! Some trees may be used for more than one thing, and some uses will have more than one tree!

Ȟaŋté
Wazí

Wáǧačhaŋ
Čhaŋšáša

Čhaŋšúška
Čhoȟwáŋžiča

Kȟáŋtahu čháŋ
Pséȟtiŋ čháŋ

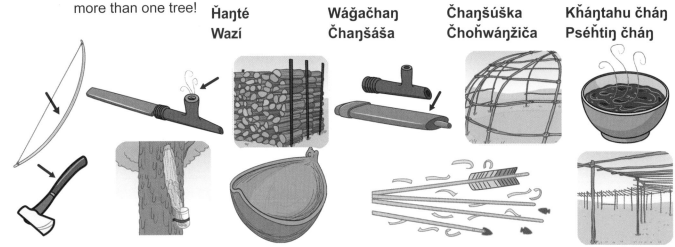

b

Bob and Lisa are writing an article about trees for the online Lakotapedia. They need to write sentences about the uses of the trees. Can you help them? Match the sentence halves correctly so that Bob and Lisa can use them in the article!

Iníthiyuktaŋ káǧapi čháŋna šna	pséȟtiŋ čháŋ ilágyapi.
Čhaŋhaŋpi káǧapi čháŋna šna	čhoȟwáŋžiča ilágyapi.
Čhaŋlí káǧapi čháŋna šna	pséȟtiŋ čháŋ ilágyapi.
Wiwáŋyaŋg wačhípi čháŋna šna	wáǧačhaŋ ilágyapi.
Waȟpé wókheya káǧapi čháŋna šna	wazí ilágyapi.
Wóžapi káǧapi čháŋna šna	kȟáŋta ilágyapi.
Itázipa káǧapi čháŋna šna	pséȟtiŋ čhaŋ naíŋš wáǧačhaŋ ilágyapi.
Waŋhíŋkpe káǧapi čháŋna šna	pséȟtiŋ čháŋ ilágyapi.
Čhaŋnúŋpa ihúpa káǧapi čháŋna šna	čhaŋšáša ilágyapi.
Wíhupa káǧapi čháŋna šna	wazí naíŋš wáǧačhaŋ ilágyapi.
Čhaŋwákšiča káǧapi čháŋna šna	pséȟtiŋ čháŋ ilágyapi.
Čhaŋáuŋpi káǧapi čháŋna šna	ȟaŋté ilágyapi.
Wazílyapi čháŋna šna	čhaŋšúška ilágyapi.

27

Iktómi is looking for sticks to make something special. Some animals in the forest give him advice on what tree to use for his project. Will he ever find the right tree?

a Skim through the story and find what he wants to make. Circle the correct picture below.

b Now, on a piece of scrap paper, make a list of all the trees Iktómi tries to use.

Aŋpétu waŋ él Iktómi waŋhíŋkpe etáŋ káǧiŋ kte. Čhaŋkhé tȟaŋkál iyáyiŋ na čháŋ etáŋ olé. Yuŋkȟáŋ hečhíŋ: "Waŋhíŋkpe kiŋ táku uŋ káǧapi so?" ečhíŋ. Yuŋkȟáŋ wábloša waŋ waŋyáŋkiŋ na heyé: "Waŋhíŋkpe káǧapi čháŋna táku čha úŋpi he?" eyá iyúŋǧe. Wábloša kiŋ heyé, "Čhaŋsákala háŋskaska úŋpi," eyá ayúpte.

Ho čha Iktómi hečhíŋ, "Oháŋ, čhaŋyáta mníŋ kte," ečhíŋ. Čhaŋmáhel í yuŋkȟáŋ gnugnúška waŋ waŋyáŋkiŋ na heyé: "Čhaŋsákala háŋskaska etáŋ owále, waŋhíŋkpe waštéšte etáŋ wakáǧiŋ kte ȟčiŋ," eyé.

Yuŋkȟáŋ gnugnúška kiŋ heyé: "Óčhičiyiŋ kte, kál kȟáŋtahu čháŋ kiŋ kaná uŋkíču kte," eyá ayúpte. Čhaŋkhé yápi na kȟáŋta čhaŋsákala eyá ičúpi.

Yuŋkȟáŋ tȟáȟča waŋ Iktó waŋyáŋkiŋ na heyé: "Iktó, čhaŋsákala kiŋ hená líla eháš pȟaŋšpȟáŋžela yeló," eyé. Heháŋl tȟáȟča kiŋ heyé: "Óčhičiyiŋ kte, kál wáǧačhaŋ kiŋ kaná uŋpáhi kte," eyé. Čhaŋkhé yápi na wáǧačhaŋ čhaŋsákala eyá pahípi.

Yuŋkȟáŋ pȟahíŋ waŋ Iktó waŋyáŋkiŋ na él í. "Iktó, čhaŋsákala kiŋ hená líla eháš šokšóke ló," eyé. Heháŋl pȟahíŋ kiŋ heyé: "Óčhičiyiŋ kte, kál ȟaŋté čháŋ kiŋ kaná uŋkíču kte," eyé. Čhaŋkhé yápi na ȟaŋté čhaŋsákala eyá ičúpi.

Yuŋkȟáŋ igmútȟaŋka waŋ Iktó waŋyáŋkiŋ na heyé: "Iktó, čhaŋsákala kiŋ hená líla eháš škoškópe ló," eyé. Heháŋl igmútȟaŋka kiŋ heyé: "Óčhičiyiŋ kte, kál čhaŋšúška čháŋ kiŋ kaná uŋpáhi kte," eyé. Čhaŋkhé yápi na čhaŋšúška čhaŋsákala eyá pahípi.

Yuŋkȟáŋ matȟó waŋ Iktó waŋyáŋkiŋ na heyé: "Iktó, čhaŋsákala kiŋ hená líla eháš pteptéčela yeló," eyé. Heháŋl matȟó kiŋ heyé: "Óčhičiyiŋ kte, kál pséȟtiŋ čháŋ kiŋ kaná uŋ uŋkáǧiŋ kte," eyé. Čhaŋkhé yápi na pséȟtiŋ čhaŋsákala eyá kaksápi kte, éyaš pséȟtiŋ čháŋ k'uŋ akáŋ kȟaŋǧí waŋ yaŋkíŋ na heyé: "Iktó, pséȟtiŋ čháŋ kiŋ lé mitȟáwa yeló. Čhič'ú kte šni yeló," eyé.

28 Match the animals with the trees each one recommends to Iktomi.

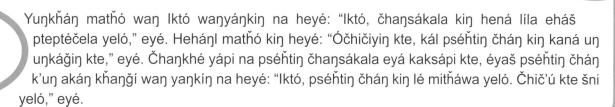

gnugnúška   pséȟtiŋ čhaŋ
tȟáȟča   čhaŋšúška
pȟahíŋ   wáǧačhaŋ
igmútȟaŋka   ȟaŋté čháŋ
matȟó   kȟáŋta čháŋ

29 There is no way Iktó can use the first four kinds of sticks! Why is that? Can you write a sentence about what he would say for each kind of stick, following the model? Write your sentences on a piece of scrap paper.

_____ čhaŋsákala kiŋ líla eháš _____ čhaŋkhé tókȟa ilágwaye šni.

<u>Kȟáŋta</u> čhaŋsákala kiŋ líla eháš <u>pȟaŋšpȟáŋžela</u> čhaŋkhé tókȟa ilágwaye šni.

30 Look at the last paragraph and circle the correct choice or choices for each question.

a Táku čháŋ uŋ-phíča he?
     wazí čháŋ   pséȟtiŋ čháŋ   wáǧačhaŋ

b Wamákȟaškaŋ kiŋ tukté waŋží Iktó wókiyaka he?
- Matȟó waŋ Iktó okíyake.
- Kȟaŋǧí waŋ Iktó okíyake.
- Šuŋǧíla waŋ Iktó okíyake.

č Táku wamákȟaškaŋ čháŋ kiŋ hé akáŋl yaŋká he?
- Matȟó waŋ čháŋ kiŋ hé akáŋl yaŋké.
- Kȟaŋǧí waŋ čháŋ kiŋ hé akáŋl yaŋké.
- Šuŋǧíla waŋ čháŋ kiŋ hé akáŋl yaŋké.

e Tákuwe Iktó čháŋ kiŋ hé ičú šni he?
- Ičhíŋ líla eháš sutá.
- Ičhíŋ líla eháš pȟaŋšpȟáŋžela.
- Ičhíŋ kȟaŋǧí kiŋ tȟáwa.

31 Do you know the word **kȟáŋta**? Listen and try to say it. Can you say the other words just as well? Try them, too!

Kȟ kȟáŋta

kȟolá, kȟúŋšitku, kȟoškálaka, okȟáte, ómakȟa, watúkȟa, kȟalkȟáte, kȟalyé

Try to say this sentence out loud! Say it once slowly, like the recording. The second time, try to say it faster.

Kȟolá kȟó wachíŋkȟo.

32 Do you know the word **pȟahíŋ**? Listen and try to say it. Can you say the other words just as well? Try them, too!

Pȟ pȟahíŋ

pȟaŋšpȟáŋžela, pȟapȟá, pȟasú, owápȟe, mas'ápȟe, epȟé, képȟe

Try to say this sentence out loud! Say it once slowly, like the recording. The second time, try to say it faster.

Pȟahíŋ waŋ čépȟaŋši napȟéye.

33 Do you know the word **tȟatȟáŋka**? Listen and try to say it. Can you say the other words just as well? Try them, too!

Tȟ tȟatȟáŋka

tȟaŋháŋši, tȟáwa, tȟaŋkší, tȟaŋníla, tȟaspáŋ, tȟašúpa, tȟéča, tȟéhaŋ, tȟotȟó

Try to say this sentence out loud! Say it once slowly, like the recording. The second time, try to say it faster.

Tȟaŋkší watȟótȟo eyá tȟebyé.

Review Quiz

1 Some of the children want to do various activities, but they don't want to do them alone! How would they invite a friend to do the activities with them? How would the friend respond? Can you fill in the speech bubbles for each child, according to the pictures?

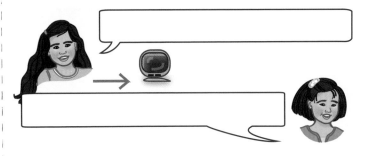
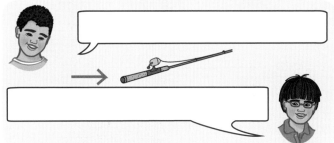

2 Now the children are telling their teacher about what they are doing. Can you fill in these speech bubbles according to the picture?

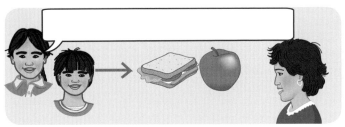
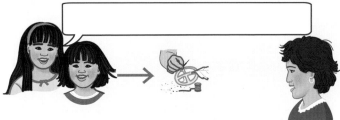

3 Can you change the "I" form of the verb to the "you and I" form? See how many you can do without looking back at the unit!

mawáni   _____

walówaŋ   _____

owále   _____

slolwáye   _____

waíŋmnaŋke _____

íblotake   _____

uŋmáspe   _____

4 Matȟó's puppy chewed some of the notes he was making for his tree guide! Can you help him rewrite the sentences that he needs to use? For each one, use all of the elements listed, and write Matȟó a correct Lakota sentence he can use!

 / ȟóta / lé

_____

 / háŋskA / lé

_____

 / pȟéstola / lená

_____

 / gmigméla / lená

_____

5 The children are playing a word game. One child says he or she is looking for something soft. The other child suggests a pillow! Look at the example cartoon, and draw your own cartoon conversations, using these other words:

 Táku waŋží pȟáŋžela čha owále.

Ipáhiŋ waŋží ičú wo.

sutá	tké	šóke
škópe	owótȟaŋla	pȟéstola
kap'óžela	zípela	

> **Mike:** Háu James, tókhiya lá he?
> **James:** Kaká thí kiŋ ektá blé.
> Ohúŋkakaŋ etáŋ oyákiŋ kte.
> **Mike:** Uŋyíŋ kta he?
> **James:** Oháŋ, uŋyíŋ kte, éyaš
> uŋkínaȟni kte héčha, oíyokpas áye.

1 Read the first part of the conversation above and look at the picture. Then, answer the questions below by circling the correct choice.

a What are Mike and James planning to do?

a. Listen to stories b. Play basketball č. Ride horses

b Which word in the sentence you circled means "stories"?
Can you write that word here? _____

2 Now, read through the above dialogue again. Can you answer all the questions?

a James tȟuŋkášitku kiŋ waŋglág yá he?
                                    Háŋ / Hiyá

b Waŋná híŋhaŋni he?   Háŋ / Hiyá

č Mike íŋš-eyá yá he?   Háŋ / Hiyá

3 Can you match these words with their dictionary form? If there are some words you don't know, look them up in the dictionary.

loyáčhiŋ	čhépA
uŋyíŋ	čhaŋzékA
lá	ȟ'aŋhí
húnistake	ináȟni
húmastake	ločhíŋ
wayáta	yÁ
mačhépe	čhuwíta
lowáčhiŋ	ȟwá
mačhúwita	watúkȟa
ničhépe	hústakA
mačháŋzeke	wótA
ničháŋzeke	
niȟ'áŋhi	
uŋkínaȟni	
maȟwá	
wamátukȟa	

4 Now read through these questions, then read the second part of Mike and James' conversation. Can you answer all the questions?

a Mike ločhíŋ he?   Háŋ / Hiyá

b James íŋš-eyá ločhíŋ he?   Háŋ / Hiyá

č Mike čhaŋzéka he?   Háŋ / Hiyá

e James čhaŋzéka he?   Háŋ / Hiyá

Mike: Huští, líla lowáčhiŋ.
James: Wáŋ, óhiŋniyaŋ loyáčhiŋ s'a. Líglila wayáte s'a háŋtaŋš ničhépiŋ kte.
Mike: Níš ničhépiŋ kte, míš mačhépiŋ kte šni.
James: Čhaŋzéke šni yo!
Mike: Hiyá, mačháŋzeke šni, íŋšé ówacháŋhaŋ epȟé.

5 Next, read through these questions and read the third part of the dialogue. Can you answer all the questions?

Mike: Áta niȟ'áŋhi yeló. Ináȟni yo.
James: Wamátukȟa na húmastake.
Mike: Óhiŋniyaŋ wanítukȟa na húnistake.
James: Nakúŋ mačhúwita na maȟwá.
Mike: Ináȟni yo. Ȟ'aŋhíya maúŋni háŋtaŋš niȟwá na ničhúwita kte šni.

a James watúkȟa he?   Háŋ / Hiyá

b James hústaka he?   Háŋ / Hiyá

č Mike watúkȟa he?   Háŋ / Hiyá

e James čhuwíta he?   Háŋ / Hiyá

g Mike ȟwá he?   Háŋ / Hiyá

6 Bonus Challenge! Can you figure these out? Read the whole dialogue again, and fill in the missing words.

Mike: Kaká thí kiŋ ektá _____ .
James: Líla wayáte háŋtaŋš _____ kte.
Mike: Ȟ'aŋhíya maúŋni háŋtaŋš _____ kte šni.

7 Mike and James walked a long way! Now they are tired, and have some other problems. Can you give them advice on what would make them feel better? First, match the complaint with the thing that might help. Then, match the item with the command you would give James or Mike.

Líla ímapuze.

Húmastake

Kitáŋla wamáyazaŋ.

Líla napé mašápe.

Líla mačhúwita.

Líla maǧáŋ.

Akíh'aŋmat'e.

Líla omákħate.

Mnikápħopapi waŋží ičú we.

Oákaŋke waŋží ičú wo/we.

Šiná waŋží ičú wo/we.

Pħežúta waŋží ičú wo/we.

Aǧúyapi waŋží ičú wo/we.

Mní etáŋ ičú wo/we.

Haípažaža waŋží ičú wo/we.

Wíglasto waŋží ičú wo/we.

8 Now, give your classmates some helpful advice! Your teacher will give you a role play card with an imaginary problem. Stand in a circle with your classmates. Tell your problem to someone, and they will give you advice. Follow the advice about what to take.

10 Get in a small group with some of your classmates. Take turns miming each of the problems. Can your classmates correctly guess your problem? Can they remember what advice to give you?

Eháŋuŋ, ínipuze. Mnikápħopapi waŋží ičú wo/we.

9 Summer is doing her homework! Can you help her match the dictionary form to the "I" form and the "You" form? Draw lines to match.

húmastake	húnistake	ípuzA
wamáyazaŋ	ínipuza	hústakA
mašápe	waníyazaŋ	čhuwíta
mačhúwita	nišápe	wayázaŋ
maǧáŋ	oníkħate	akíh'aŋt'A
akíh'aŋmat'e	akíh'aŋnit'e	okħátA
omákħate	ničhúwita	napé šápA
ímapuza	niǧáŋ	ǧáŋ

11 Oh no! Your classmates all have problems!

Your teacher will tell you about several class-mates. With your team, figure out the right response, like the model. If your response is correct, your team gets a point! The team with the most points wins!

Ípuzapi.

Mnikápȟopapi waŋžígži wičhák'u po/pe.

12 Mike and James are happy now, because they are sitting down, and Grandpa is telling a story! Read the beginning of Grandpa's story and look at the pictures below. Then, answer the questions.

Iktómi ománi yá-he. Táku waŋ naȟ'úŋ.
Ptepȟá waŋ waŋyáŋke.
Mahél itȟúŋkala čha wačhípi na lowáŋpi.
Iktómi heyé: "Míš-eyá wawáčhi kte," eyé.
Natá kiŋ pathíma hiyúkiya yuŋkȟáŋ oyátȟake.

a Iktómi táku tókȟuŋ he?

b Iktómi táku čha waŋyáŋka he?

č Tuwé čha wačhípi he?

itȟúŋkala   tȟatȟáŋka   gnugnúška

e Iktó táku čha úŋ he? Táku čha pȟóštaŋ he?
- wapȟóštaŋ waŋ
- ptepȟá kiŋ
- wápaha waŋ

13 Iktómi still has the skull on his head! And now he is meeting other animals that he can't see! Read the next part of the story, and answer the questions.

a Make a list on scratch paper. What body parts does the animal have? (Hint: there are 6 of them).

b What word does the animal use to indicate that it has a certain body part? Write it here:

_____

č What word does the animal use to indicate that it does NOT have a certain body part? Write it here:

_____

e What word do you use to ask "Do you have?" with body parts? What word does Iktó use?
Write it here: _____

g Can you guess what animal this is?
Circle the correct choice below and then write it into the end of the story.

heȟáka   ptéȟčaka   waŋblí

Iktómi: Nitáku he?

?:   Wamákȟaškaŋ hemáčha.

Iktómi: Hú nitóna he?

?:   Hú matópa.

Iktómi: Wíyaka niyúkȟaŋ he?

?:   Hiyá, wíyaka mawániča.

Iktómi: Sišáke niyúkȟaŋ he?

?:   Háŋ, sišáke mayúkȟe.

Iktómi: Apȟéyohaŋ niyúkȟaŋ he?

?:   Hiyá, apȟéyohaŋ mawániča.

Iktómi: Siŋté niyúkȟaŋ he?

?:   Háŋ, siŋté mayúkȟe.

Iktómi: Hé niyúkȟaŋ he?

?:   Háŋ, hé mayúkȟe.

Iktómi: Híŋ niyúkȟaŋ he?

?:   Háŋ, híŋ mayúkȟe.

Iktómi: Hí niyúkȟaŋ he?

?:   Háŋ, hí mayúkȟe.

Iktómi: Heȟáka heníčha he?

?:   Hiyá, heȟáka hemáčha šni.

Iktómi: _____ heníčha he?

?:   Háŋ, _____ hemáčha.

---

14 # Abléza po!

1) The buffalo is talking about his tail. Which of the sentences below is correct? Cross out the incorrect sentence.

Siŋté mayúkȟe.   **Siŋté waŋ bluhá.**

2) Bob is talking about the buffalo's tail. Which of the sentences below is correct? Cross out the incorrect sentence.

Siŋté yukȟé.   **Siŋté waŋ yuhá.**

3) Now, the buffalo is talking about not having wings. How does he say this in Lakota? Cross out the incorrect sentence.

Ȟupáhu mawániče.   **Ȟupáhu bluhá šni.**

4) The buffalo is talking about his four legs. How does he talk about them in Lakota? Cross out the incorrect sentence:

Hú matópa.   **Hú tópa bluhá.**

15 Iktómi, who still has a skull on his head, meets up with another creature. Look at the picture, and fill in the blanks in the story below.

Iktómi: Nitáku he?
siŋtéȟla: Wamákȟaškaŋ hemácha.
Iktómi: Hú nitóna he?
siŋtéȟla: Hóȟ, hú mawániče.
Iktómi: Wíyaka niyúkȟaŋ he?
siŋtéȟla: Hiyá, wíyaka mawániče.
Iktómi: Híŋ _____ he?
siŋtéȟla: _____, híŋ _____.

Iktómi: Hí _____ he?
siŋtéȟla: _____, hí _____.
Iktómi: Ištá _____ he?
siŋtéȟla: _____, ištá _____.
Iktómi: Hé _____ he?
siŋtéȟla: _____, hé _____.
Iktómi: Hú _____ he?
siŋtéȟla: _____, hú _____.

16 Iktómi is still walking around, with his head in a skull, meeting various creatures. What creature does he meet up with next? Read the next part of the story, and find out. Write the name of the animal into the end of the story below.

Iktómi: Háu, nitáku he?
? :   Ziŋtkála hemácha.
Iktómi: Hú nitóna he?
? :   Hú manúŋpa.
Iktómi: Pȟasú toníkča he?
? :   Pȟasú mazí na maškópe.
Iktómi: Siŋtúpi toníkča he?
? :   Siŋtúpi maháŋskiŋ na masáŋ.
Iktómi: Šaké toníkča he?
? :   Šaké masápsapiŋ na mapȟépȟe.
Iktómi: Natá toníkča he?
? :   Natá masáŋ.

Iktómi: Ȟupáhu toníkča he?
? :   Ȟupáhu maháŋskaska na matȟáŋkiŋkiŋyaŋ.
Iktómi: Sí toníkča he?
? :   Sí mazízi na mayúȟ'iȟ'i.
Iktómi: Ištá toníkča he?
? :   Ištá mačíkčik'ala na magmígmigma.
Iktómi: Nakpá _____ he?
? :   Nakpá mawániče.
Iktómi: _____ heníčha he?
?:   Háŋ, _____ hemácha.

17 **Abléza po!**

1) How does Iktómi ask the bird the following question: "What are your wings like?" Find it in the dialogue above and write it here:

_____

2) How does the bird say "My wings are long," in the story? Write it here:

_____

18 Iktómi still hasn't managed to pull the skull off his head! So as he's walking, he meets another creature he can't see. Can you help finish the story by using the words from the list? Be careful! Words may be used more than once.

maháŋske	~~mayúȟ'i~~	magmígmigma
maháŋskaska	mawániče	maptéčela
matópa	matȟáŋka	mapȟéstola
~~maǧí~~	matȟáŋkiŋkiŋyaŋ	

Iktómi: Nitáku he?
gnaška: Wamákȟaškaŋ hemáčha.
Iktómi: Hú nitóna he?
gnaška: Hú matópa.
Iktómi: Čheží toníkča he?
gnaška: Čheží _____ .
Iktómi: Hú toníkča he?
gnaška: Hú _____ .
Iktómi: Hú nitóna he?
gnaška: Hú _____ .
Iktómi: Há toníkča he?
gnaška: Há __maǧí__ na __mayúȟ'i__ .

Iktómi: Hí toníkča he?
gnaška: Hí _____ .
Iktómi: Í toníkča he?
gnaška: Í _____ .
Iktómi: Ištá toníkča he?
gnaška: Ištá _____ na _____ .
Iktómi: Siŋté toníkča he?
gnaška: Siŋté _____ .
Iktómi: Phuté toníkča he?
gnaška: Phuté _____ na _____ .
Iktómi: Hé toníkča he?
gnaška: Hé _____ .

19 To the right are some of the words that I used when describing myself. What is the affix that I used to show that I was talking about my own body parts? Underline it in each of the words. When you are done, decide which of the words talk about body parts that are plural (more than one). Circle them.

maháŋske	____	maǧí	____
matópa	____	mapȟéstostola	____
matȟáŋka	____	matȟáŋkiŋkiŋyaŋ	____
magmígmigma	____	maptéčela	____
maháŋskaska	____	maptéptečela	____
magmígme	____	maǧíǧi	____
mayúȟ'i	____	mapȟéstola	____

20 What body parts do each of these animals have? Fill in the column for each animal below using these words. Some parts may be used more than once, some parts not at all.

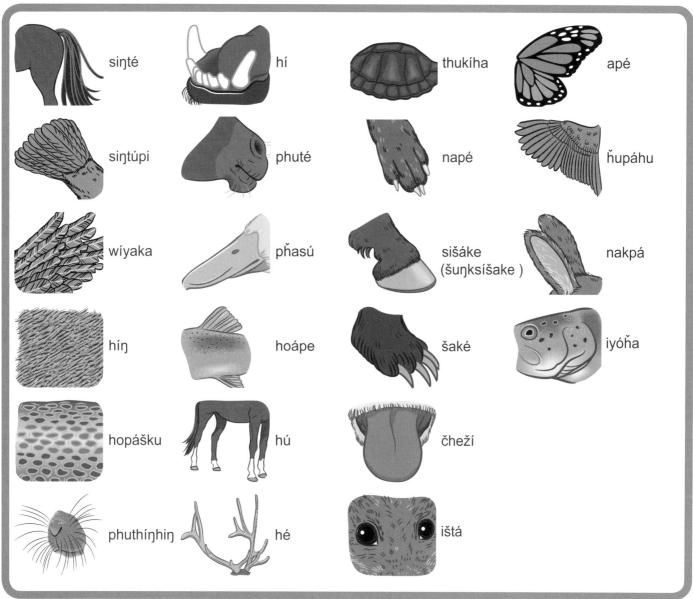

siŋté — hí — thukíha — apé
siŋtúpi — phuté — napé — ȟupáhu
wíyaka — pȟasú — sišáke (šuŋksíšake) — nakpá
híŋ — hoápe — šaké — iyóȟa
hopášku — hú — čheží
phuthíŋhiŋ — hé — ištá

 heȟáka

 uŋkčékhiȟa

 pȟatkáša

 hoǧáŋ

21 Now, let's play a guessing game with your classmates! First, get in a big circle. Then, your teacher will give you a picture of a bird or animal. Don't show it to anybody! They have to guess what you are!

Your teacher will start off. You can ask him or her questions, like the model. See if you can guess which bird or animal he or she is! Then, try to ask questions and guess your classmates' animals.

> Wamákȟaškaŋ hemáčha.

> Hí niyúkȟaŋ he?

> Háŋ, hí mayúkȟe.

> Wíyaka niyúkȟaŋ he?

> Hiyá, wíyaka mawániče.

22 Write a description of an animal using six sentences on scratch paper. Use the example sentences below to help you think about the possibilities!

Siŋté mayúkȟe.

Nakpá mačíkčik'ala.

Hú mahánskaska.

Hé mawániče.

Hú matópa

Siŋté mahánske.

Hiŋ maǧí.

23 Now, read your description to a partner. He/she will guess what animal you are, as in the model sentences below.

> _____ heníčha he?

> Hiyá, _____ hemáčha šni.

> Háŋ, _____ hemáčha.

24 **a** Iktómi is still walking about, and meeting various creatures! Listen to the conversations he has, and number the birds/animals in the order he meets them.

b 🔊 Next, your teacher will play Iktómi's conversations for you one by one. For each conversation, put a check mark on or next to each body part that Iktómi mentions, and that the bird or animal has.

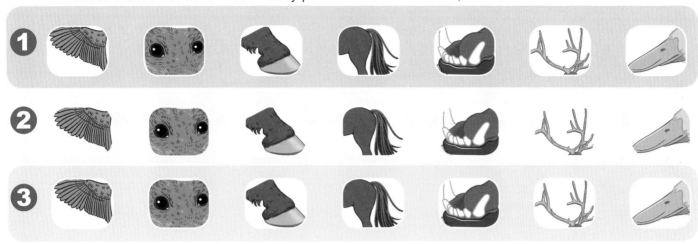

č Now, your teacher will play each conversation for you a third time. For each pair, circle the correct choice as Iktómi describes it for that animal.

25 🔊 What DON'T the animals have? What body parts does Iktómi mention that the bird or animal does not have? For each animal, listen to the conversation, and circle the picture or pictures of what Iktómi asks about, but that the bird/animal says it doesn't have.

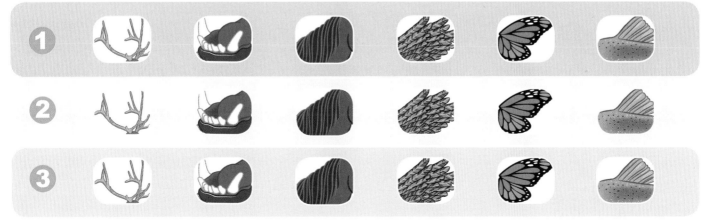

26 Do you know how to say these letters? You haven't heard them in English, because they're special in Lakota! Listen to your teacher or the recording, and try to make the sound yourself. Then, practice your pronunciation using the word samples for each sound.

Finally, try the tongue twisters on the next page. How clearly can you say them?

①  t': t'á, t'é, iȟát'a, t'at'á, t'at'áič'iya, t'ečá, t'osyéla, t'uŋgyá

②  č': č'ó, č'oyéla, eíč'iya, kič'úŋ, kač'úŋ, naíč'ižiŋ, óič'iye

③  k': k'á, k'ú, k'éyaš, k'íŋ, k'ó, k'uŋ, uŋk'úŋpi

④  p': p'ó, p'oyéla, p'é, p'éčhaŋ, čhap'óle, haŋp'íkčeka, kap'óžela, wanáp'iŋ

⑤  ȟ': ȟ'áŋ, kaȟ'ól, ȟ'aŋhí, ȟ'aŋȟ'áŋ s'e, ȟ'eȟ'éyela, ȟ'úŋt'e

⑥  s': s'a, s'e, s'íŋ, s'elé, s'íŋs'iŋyaŋ, as'íŋ, atáŋs'e, ahíyokas'iŋ

⑦  š': š'á, š'é, š'éš'e, yuš'íŋš'iŋ, waš'áke, iš'óš'oya, mniš'éš'e

27 Try these tongue twisters! Watch out - they're difficult to say, so pronounce them carefully! You might have to try several times before you get it.

1. Míyoglas'iŋ waŋ él waŋíč'iglake.
2. Matȟápiȟ'a waŋ khes'ámna waŋ mas'ákipȟe.
3. Šič'éku kiŋ haŋp'íkčeka s'amná eyá k'ú.
4. P'ó čha kap'óšp'ožela máni.
5. Watúkȟa čha t'at'áič'iye.
6. Khes'ámna kiŋ iglúš'iŋš'iŋ.
7. Khes'ámna kiŋ šič'éku kiŋ iš'óš'oya yuš'íŋš'iŋ.
8. Khes'ámna kiŋ s'íŋs'iŋyaŋ wóte.
9. Khes'ámna waŋ čík'ala čha líla waȟ'áŋič'ila.
10. Matȟápiȟ'a waŋ khes'ámna waŋ iš'óš'oya mas'ákipȟe.

Review Quiz

1 Some of the children had problems today! Can you guess what the problems were from the solutions? Write what each child would say, like the example:

Tȟašína mnikápȟopapi waŋ ičú. ---> _Líla omákȟate!_

Lisa pȟežúta waŋ ičú. ---> _____

Kimi wíglasto waŋ ičú. ---> _____

Mike šiná waŋ ičú. ---> _____

Matȟó mní eyá ičú. ---> _____

James oákaŋke waŋ ičú. ---> _____

Summer aǧúyapi waŋ ičú. ---> _____

2 Now, can you write the questions that you might ask someone for the situations above, like the example? Write your questions on scrap paper.
Example: _Oníkȟata he?_

3 Can you match up these sentences? Draw lines.

Líla okȟáte!   Oákaŋke waŋží k'ú wo!

Líla čhuwítapi!   Šiná waŋží wičhák'u wo!

Líla ǧáŋ!   Aǧúyapi waŋží wičhák'u wo!

Líla ípuzapi!   Pȟežúta etáŋ wičhák'u wo!

Líla hústake!   Mnikápȟopapi waŋží k'ú wo!

Líla wayázaŋpi!   Wíglasto waŋží k'ú wo!

Líla ločhíŋpi!   Mní etáŋ wičhák'u wo!

4 Can you help the animals describe themselves? Write sentences to tell whether the animal speaking does or does not have the body part pictured.

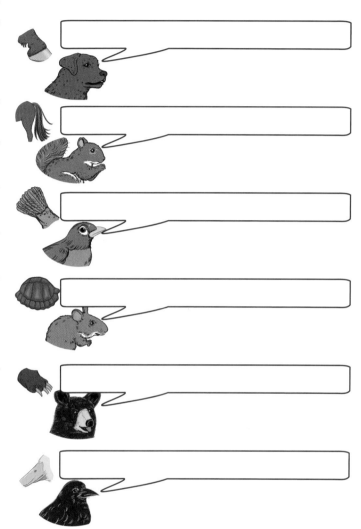

5 Can you pick the correct form? For each animal, circle the correct word in each pair.

Waŋblí:
- Siŋtúpi maháŋske / maháŋskaska.
- Sí mazí / mazízi.
- Ištá mačík'ala / mačíkčik'ala

Khéya:
- Thukíha masúta / masúksuta
- Hú maptéčela / maptéptečela
- Ištá magmígme / magmígmigme

1 Bob and Lisa have gotten really interested in animals, and want to learn more about them. What do they do? Skim through the comic and find the answer to the first question below. Then, check your answer with your classmates and your teacher. Next, skim through for the answer to the second question, and check with classmates, and so on.

a Bob é na Lisa táku olépi he?

b Bob é na Lisa tókhiya yápi kta he?
_____ waŋ ektá yápi kte.

č Bob é na Lisa táku wamákȟaškaŋ waŋyáŋkapi he?
_____ waŋ waŋyáŋkapi.

Bob, ták tókȟanuŋ kta he?

Pahá-ta mníŋ kte.

Ohán, uŋyíŋ kte.

Tȟáȟča oyé owále kte.

Čhó, uŋkóle kte.

Ká pahá kiŋ ektá uŋyíŋ kte.

Ohán, uŋk'íŋyaŋkiŋ kte.

Wáŋ ká waŋ! Čhaŋhá kiŋ abléza yo.

Táku čha čhaŋhá kiŋ tȟebyá he?

Tȟáȟča héčhuŋpi okíhipi šni, ičhíŋ líla waŋkátuya.

Má! Čhaŋwáŋkal táku waŋ yaŋké. Pȟahíŋ s'eléčheča.

Itéšniyaŋ! Pȟahíŋ kiŋ čhaŋwáŋkal alípi séče éyaš tóhaŋni héčhel waŋbláke šni.

Míš-eyá. Čhaŋ-álipi kiŋ oslólwaye šni.

Pȟahíŋ kiŋ čhaŋhá ečéla yútapi kéčhaŋni he?

Waníyetu čháŋna šna čhaŋhá ečéla yútapi kéčhaŋmi.

Ho čha blokétu čháŋna táku čha yútapi kéčhaŋni he?

Táku yútapi ka héči!? Ho éyaš wówapi waŋ él pȟahíŋ kiŋ ečhétkiya waúŋyawapi kte.

Eháŋuŋ, blokétu čháŋna pȟahíŋ kiŋ čhaŋwápe é na waptáye yútapi.

Ho na haŋhépi čháŋna wóyute ignípi, aŋpétu čháŋna ištíŋmapi kéyapi.

2 Can you figure out the meaning of **thébyA** from what Bob and Lisa say, and from the pictures? Circle the best choice.

it ate it   it scratched it   it burned it

3 Can you figure out the meaning of these words by using your dictionary? Check the meaning of the underlined words, and then answer "**Háŋ**" or "**Hiyá**" for each question.

A) Pȟahíŋ kiŋ hé <u>waŋkátuya</u> yaŋká he? _____

B) Pȟahíŋ kiŋ hé <u>hukȟúčiyela</u> yaŋká he? _____

4 Read the comic strip carefully to answer these questions. Base your answer on what Bob and Lisa say.

a Táku čha čhaŋhá kiŋ tȟebyá he?
_____ waŋ čhaŋhá kiŋ tȟebyé.

čhápa   tȟáȟča   pȟahíŋ

b Bob tóhaŋȟčiŋ pȟahíŋ waŋží čhaŋwáŋkal yaŋká čha waŋyáŋka he?   háŋ / hiyá

č Lisa pȟahíŋ kiŋ čhaŋ-álipi kiŋ oslólya he?
háŋ / hiyá

e Bob Lisa kičhí tuktél pȟahíŋ kiŋ ečhétkiya wayáwapi kta he?
- owáyawa kiŋ él
- wówapi thípi waŋ él
- wówapi waŋ él

5 Keep reading, and answer these questions by writing your answer after each question.

1. Waníyetu čháŋna pȟahíŋ kiŋ táku yútapi he?
_____

2. Blokétu čháŋna pȟahíŋ kiŋ táku yútapi he?
_____

6 Bob é na Lisa táku čha yawápi he?
- wówapi
- wičhítenaškaŋškaŋ
- wótȟaŋiŋ wówapi

7 **1** Look through the comic strip, find the "you and I" verbs, and write them below.

uŋyíŋ _____ waŋyáŋkA

_____ íŋyaŋkA

_____ olé

_____ yÁ

_____ éoyakA

2 Now, draw lines to match the first dual verbs with its dictionary form in the next column.

8 **a** What do you want to do this weekend? Your teacher will give you a role play card. Walk around the room, and invite your classmates until you find someone who will do the activity with you!

Wakhúl uŋyíŋ kte.

Oháŋ, wakhúl uŋyíŋ kte. / Hiyá, wakhúl uŋyíŋ kte šni.

b Now, take out a piece of scrap paper and write a sentence about what you and your classmate will be doing this weekend!

Wóuŋglakapi kte. _____

9 Here is the first paragraph of the encyclopedia entry that Bob and Lisa read. Skim through the first paragraph, and circle all the body parts mentioned. There are at least ten.

Pȟahíŋ kiŋ tókhel owáŋyaŋkapi he?

Tóhaŋ ȟčiŋ pȟahíŋ waŋží waŋláke s'eléčheča. Pȟahíŋ kiŋ gmigméla owáŋyaŋkapi. Natá čík'alapi na nakpá čikčík'alapi. Phuté ptéčelapi na hú pteptéčelapi éyaš š'agš'ákapi. Ité sápapi na nakúŋ ištá sapsápapi. Ištá mimémelapi na čikčík'alapi na nakúŋ í čík'alapi. Napsú tópapi na siókaza záptaŋpi. Híŋ ǧiǧípi naíŋš ȟolȟótapi. Líla hiŋšmášmapi na pȟahíŋ pȟepȟé ótapi. Siŋté háŋskapi na šaké háŋskaskapi na škoškópapi. Naháŋ nakúŋ pȟahíŋ kiŋ šičámnapi.

10 How do we describe porcupines? Read the first paragraph, and match the body part or quality with the correct picture. Write the word that describes this body part in the blank, then circle the image that best matches.

 a [_____]

b [_____]

 č [_____]

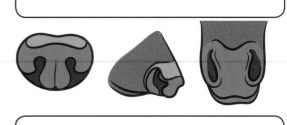

e [_____]

g [_____]

ǧ

h

ȟ

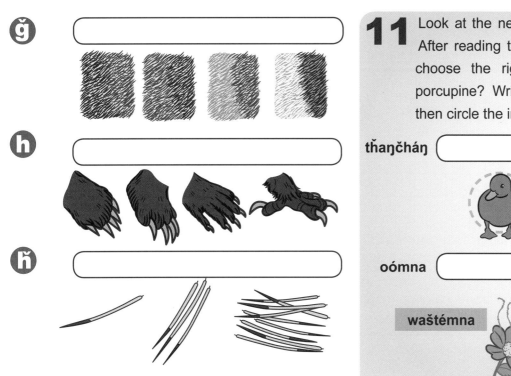

11 Look at the new words and the pictures. After reading the entry from #9, can you choose the right way to describe the porcupine? Write the word in the blank, then circle the image that best matches.

tȟaŋčháŋ

oómna

waštémna   **šičámna**

12 Now read the next part of the encyclopedia entry about porcupines. Can you match each of the sentences with the correct picture? Draw lines to match them!

Pȟahíŋ kiŋ tókhel ophíič'iyapi kiŋ lé é.

Aŋpétu čháŋna šna pȟahíŋ kiŋ naȟmá ištíŋmapi na haŋhépi čháŋna šnaománipi na šna wóyute ignípi. Pȟahíŋ kiŋ líla taŋyáŋ čhaŋ-álipi na waŋkátuya čháŋ akáŋlkaŋl šna yaŋkápi s'a. Nakúŋ pȟahíŋ kiŋ taŋyáŋkel nuŋwáŋpi. Pȟahíŋ wíŋyela kiŋ čhiŋčála waŋžígžila yuhápi.

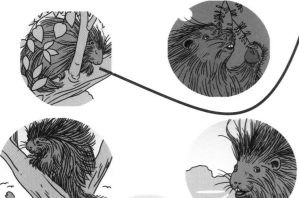

1. Aŋpétu čháŋna šna pȟahíŋ kiŋ naȟmá ištíŋmapi.

2. Haŋhépi čháŋna šna pȟahíŋ kiŋ kiktá úŋpi na šna wóyute ignípi.

3. Pȟahíŋ kiŋ líla taŋyáŋ čhaŋ-álipi.

4. Pȟahíŋ kiŋ čhaŋ-wáŋkalkal šna yaŋkápi s'a.

5. Nakúŋ pȟahíŋ kiŋ taŋyáŋkel nuŋwáŋpi.

6. Ptaŋyétu čháŋna šna pȟahíŋ kiŋ hóniskoskopi.

7. Pȟahíŋ wíŋyela kiŋ čhiŋčála waŋžígžila šna yuhápi.

13 Abléza po!

1) How do we talk about one specific animal? How do we talk about all of the animals of one kind, in general? Can you match the Lakota sentences with the English translation?

Šúŋkawakȟáŋ kiŋ lé taŋyáŋ íŋyaŋke.
Šúŋkawakȟáŋ kiŋ taŋtáŋyaŋ íŋyaŋkapi.

Šúŋkawakȟáŋ kiŋ lé wayášla.
Šúŋkawakȟáŋ kiŋ wayášlapi.

Horses run well.
This horse runs well.

This horse is grazing.
Horses graze.

2) In English we say "Horses graze." In Lakota, we say, "**Šúŋkawakȟáŋ kiŋ wayášlapi.**"
What extra word is needed in Lakota? Write it here: _____

14 **a** Now let's talk about some other animals! Grasshoppers jump; bears hibernate. What about the animals below? Can you complete the sentences below, according to the pictures?

1. **Heȟáka** **kiŋ** _wayášlapi_ .
2. **Ptéȟčaka** **kiŋ** _____ .
3. **Šúŋka** _____ _____ .
4. **Hoǧáŋ** _____ _____ .

5. **Zičá** _____ _____ .
6. **Maštíŋčala** _____ _____ .
7. **Zuzéča** _____ _____ .
8. **Ziŋtkála** _____ _____ .

b Take out a piece of scrap paper. Can you use the same verbs to talk about what other animals do in general? Write two more sentences!

15 Abléza po!

How do we talk about the ears of a single, particular porcupine? How do we talk about the ears of porcupines in general? Write the word "**waŋžíla**" ('a single one') next to the sentence about one particular porcupine. Write the word "**iyúha**" ('all') next to the sentence about porcupines in general.

Pȟahíŋ kiŋ lé nakpá čikčík'ala.   **Pȟahíŋ kiŋ nakpá čikčík'alapi.**

16 Maťhó has a new colt! He named it Ťhaté. He is telling Bob that his colt is special, but Bob is not so sure! Can you help Bob and Maťhó finish their sentences?

What would we use to say that a specific animal, like Ťhaté, has a long tail? What would we use to say that a specific animal has long legs? How would we say that all horses have long tails?

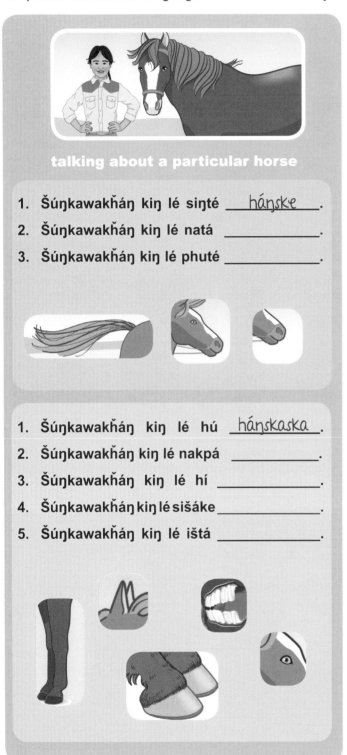

talking about a particular horse

1. Šúŋkawakȟáŋ kiŋ lé siŋté ___hánske___.
2. Šúŋkawakȟáŋ kiŋ lé natá _____.
3. Šúŋkawakȟáŋ kiŋ lé phuté _____.

1. Šúŋkawakȟáŋ kiŋ lé hú ___hánskaska___.
2. Šúŋkawakȟáŋ kiŋ lé nakpá _____.
3. Šúŋkawakȟáŋ kiŋ lé hí _____.
4. Šúŋkawakȟáŋ kiŋ lé sišáke _____.
5. Šúŋkawakȟáŋ kiŋ lé ištá _____.

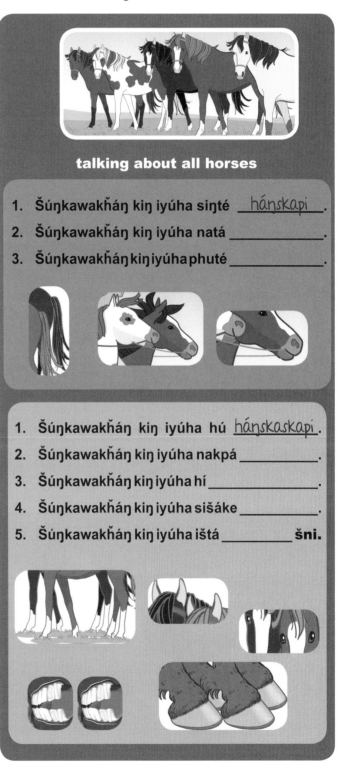

talking about all horses

1. Šúŋkawakȟáŋ kiŋ iyúha siŋté ___hánskapi___.
2. Šúŋkawakȟáŋ kiŋ iyúha natá _____.
3. Šúŋkawakȟáŋ kiŋ iyúha phuté _____.

1. Šúŋkawakȟáŋ kiŋ iyúha hú ___hánskaskapi___.
2. Šúŋkawakȟáŋ kiŋ iyúha nakpá _____.
3. Šúŋkawakȟáŋ kiŋ iyúha hí _____.
4. Šúŋkawakȟáŋ kiŋ iyúha sišáke _____.
5. Šúŋkawakȟáŋ kiŋ iyúha ištá _____ **šni.**

17 What is really special about Maťhó's colt?

Read back through the lists and write it here:_____

18 Do you know why the first sentence below has **čík'alapi** and the second has **čikčík'alapi**? Can you figure out what to write for the other pictures?

1. Itȟúŋkala kiŋ phuté čík'alapi.

2. Itȟúŋkala kiŋ ištá čikčík'alapi.

3. Šúŋkawakȟáŋ kiŋ siŋté _____.

4. Šúŋkawakȟáŋ kiŋ hú _____.

5. Pȟahíŋ kiŋ hú _____.

6. Pȟahíŋ kiŋ _____.

7. Pȟahíŋ _____ _____.

8. _____ _____ _____.

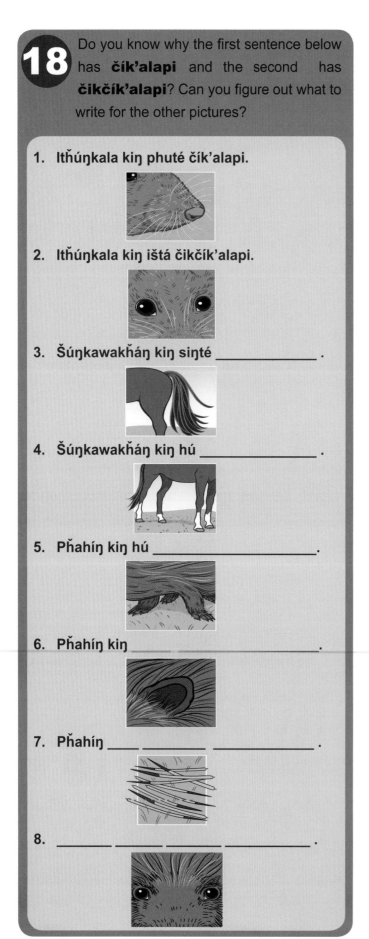

19 Bob is writing a report on porcupines. He is trying to talk about the parts of their bodies. Which words should he use? Can you help him? Decide whether porcupines have one, two or many of each body part, and then which word best describes that body part. Draw lines to match!

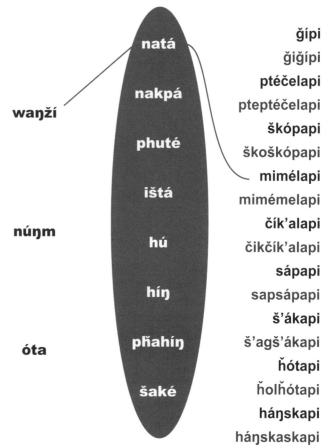

waŋží

núŋm

óta

natá
nakpá
phuté
ištá
hú
híŋ
pȟahíŋ
šaké

ǧípi
ǧiǧípi
ptéčelapi
pteptéčelapi
škópapi
škoškópapi
mimélapi
mimémelapi
čík'alapi
čikčík'alapi
sápapi
sapsápapi
š'ákapi
š'agš'ákapi
ȟótapi
ȟolȟótapi
háŋskapi
háŋskaskapi

20 Choose a type of animal from the picture to talk about. Describe the following body parts: **siŋté, hú,** and **nakpá**. Can your partner guess which one you chose?

21 Skim through the third paragraph of the encyclopedia entry below to find the answer to these two questions. Circle the word or words that gave you the answer.

1. Pȟahíŋ kiŋ tȟaló yútapi he?
2. Pȟahíŋ kiŋ watȟóka yútapi he?

Pȟahíŋ kiŋ táku yútapi he?

Pȟahíŋ kiŋ hitȟúŋka héčhapi. Wétu na blokétu čháŋna šna waȟpé na čhaŋsákala na waptáye kȟó yútapi, naíŋš táku watȟóka ke éyaš. Waníyetu čháŋna šna čhaŋhá mahétaŋhaŋ yúl awáštelakapi. Líglila ȟ'aŋhíya šna wótapi. Iyótaŋš wazí čhaŋhá mahétaŋhaŋ waštélakapi. Na nakúŋ líla mniskúya waštélakapi na wétu čháŋna čhíŋkpa na waskúyeča yútapi.

22 Read through the encyclopedia paragraph above and answer the following questions.

b First, match the word with the pictures. Then, answer the question.

Wétu čháŋna šna táku yútapi he?

a Pȟahíŋ kiŋ watȟóka yútapi. Wamákȟaškaŋ kiŋ tuktená pȟahíŋ kiŋ iyéčhel wótapi he?

itȟúŋkala

gnašká

igmú

zičá

(čhápa)

šuŋgmánitu

itȟúŋkasaŋ

waglékšuŋ

hiŋháŋ

pispíza

gnugnúška

siŋkpȟé

waȟpé
čhaŋsákala
waptáye
čhaŋhá mahétaŋhaŋ
čhíŋkpa
waskúyeča

23 Use your dictionary to look up the words **ȟ'aŋhíya** and **oȟ'áŋkȟoya**. Then answer the questions below with **háŋ** or **hiyá**.

1. Pȟahíŋ kiŋ ȟ'aŋhíya wótapi he?   Háŋ / Hiyá
2. Pȟahíŋ kiŋ oȟ'áŋkȟoya wótapi he? Háŋ / Hiyá

24 Pȟahíŋ kiŋ táku líla waštélakapi he?

1. _____

2. _____

25 We know, from reading the encyclopedia, that porcupines eat plants. Look at the image. The baby porcupine will use the following words to talk about each thing : **lé, hé, ká, lenáos, henáos, kanáos, lená, hená, kaná**. Think about how close or far the items are to him or his mother. Use the correct words to answer the questions, like the example. Hint: Check your answers in the encyclopedia article!

> Pȟahíŋ čhiŋčála kiŋ líla ločhíŋ. Pȟahíŋ kiŋ eyášna táku yútapi héči húŋku iyúŋǧe. Húŋku ayúpte.

1. Pȟahíŋ čhiŋčála:
Čhaŋsákala kiŋ lená uŋyútiŋ kta he?
Pȟahíŋ húŋku: <u>Háŋ, kaná uŋyútiŋ kte.</u>

2. Pȟahíŋ čhiŋčála:
Čhíŋkpa kiŋ kaná uŋyútiŋ kta he?
Húŋku:_____

3. Pȟahíŋ čhiŋčála:
Waptáye kiŋ lená uŋyútiŋ kta he?
Húŋku:_____

4. Pȟahíŋ čhiŋčála:
Waglúla kiŋ lenáos wičhúŋyutiŋ kta he?
Húŋku:_____

5. Pȟahíŋ čhiŋčála:
Kimímela kiŋ lenáos wičhúŋyutiŋ kta he?
Húŋku:_____

6. Pȟahíŋ čhiŋčála:
Gnugnúška kiŋ kaná wičhúŋyutiŋ kta he?
Húŋku:_____

7. Pȟahíŋ čhiŋčála:
Čhaŋšíŋ kiŋ ká uŋyútiŋ kta he?
Húŋku:_____

26 Look at the following pairs of animals and the foods they eat. Work with a partner. One of you should suggest a food for both of you to eat; the other will guess which animal you both are. See the model:

27 The last paragraph of the encyclopedia article is talking about how the Lakota used the porcupine traditionally. But the sentences got scrambled! Can you put them back in the correct order? Number the sentences!

> Pȟeží uŋyútiŋ kte.

> Eháŋuŋ, šúŋkawakȟáŋ heúŋčha.

Heháŋl pȟahíŋ pȟepȟé kiŋ yužážapi.

1 Tȟokáheya pȟahíŋ pȟepȟé kiŋ yužúŋžuŋpi.

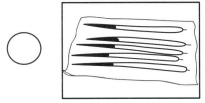

Heháŋl pȟahíŋ pȟepȟé kiŋ pusyápi.

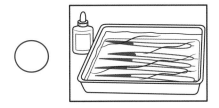

Ehákeȟčiŋ pȟahíŋ pȟepȟé kiŋ uŋ wípatȟapi.

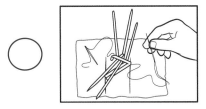

Heháŋl pȟahíŋ pȟepȟé kiŋ lulyápi.

28 a Listen to the description about this animal. Answer the questions by circling "**Háŋ**" or "**Hiyá**."

Wamákȟaškaŋ kiŋ lená hú núŋpapi he? Háŋ / (Hiyá)

1. Wamákȟaškaŋ kiŋ lená hú núŋpapi he? Háŋ / Hiyá
2. Wamákȟaškaŋ kiŋ lená hú háŋskaskapi he? Háŋ / Hiyá
3. Wamákȟaškaŋ kiŋ lená lúzahaŋpi he? Háŋ / Hiyá
4. Wamákȟaškaŋ kiŋ lená aŋpétu čháŋna šna ištíŋmapi he? Háŋ / Hiyá
5. Wamákȟaškaŋ kiŋ lená aŋpétu čháŋna šna kiktá úŋpi he? Háŋ / Hiyá
6. Wamákȟaškaŋ kiŋ lená haŋhépi čháŋna šna wígnipi he? Háŋ / Hiyá
7. Wamákȟaškaŋ kiŋ lená čhaŋ-álipi he? Háŋ / Hiyá
8. Wamákȟaškaŋ kiŋ lená ȟupáhu yukȟáŋpi he? Háŋ / Hiyá
9. Wamákȟaškaŋ kiŋ lená siŋté ptéčelapi he? Háŋ / Hiyá
10. Wamákȟaškaŋ kiŋ lená šaké yukȟáŋpi he? Háŋ / Hiyá
11. Wamákȟaškaŋ kiŋ lená waníyetu čháŋna čhuwítapi he? Háŋ / Hiyá
12. Wamákȟaškaŋ kiŋ lená hé yukȟáŋpi he? Háŋ / Hiyá
13. Wamákȟaškaŋ kiŋ lená watȟóka yútapi he? Háŋ / Hiyá

b Listen to the description of the animal again. Can you answer the questions, like the example?

Wamákȟaškaŋ kiŋ lená tákuwe táku kiŋ iyúha taŋtáŋyaŋ ómnapi he?
Pȟuté háŋskapi čha hé uŋ.

1. Wamákȟaškaŋ kiŋ lená tákuwe lúzahaŋpi he?

_____

2. Wamákȟaškaŋ kiŋ lená tákuwe kiŋyáŋpi šni he?

_____

3. Wamákȟaškaŋ kiŋ lená tákuwe waníyetu čháŋna šna čhuwítapi šni he?

_____

4. Wamákȟaškaŋ kiŋ lená tákuwe hí pȟestóstolapi he?

_____

č Listen a third time. Now can you guess what animal this is? Circle the correct choice.

29 Lisa went back in the woods to look for more tracks! Here are two paragraphs about what happened. Can you finish them? Use the words beneath each paragraph to finish.

wók'u   mnik'ú   čhašt̄ȟúŋ
yužáža   p̄ȟóskil yúze

Lisa šuŋk'óye eyá waŋyáŋka čhaŋkhé otȟáb máni. Yuŋkȟáŋ šuŋȟpála waŋ iyéye. Šuŋȟpála kiŋ líla záŋgzaŋka čha Lisa ičú na thiyáta akȟí. Šuŋȟpála kiŋ líla šápa čha Lisa _____. Šuŋȟpála kiŋ líla ločhíŋ čha Lisa _____. Šuŋȟpála kiŋ líla ípuza čha Lisa _____. Lisa šuŋȟpála kiŋ líla waštélaka čha _____. Na heháŋl Lisa šuŋȟpála kiŋ "Maȟpíya," eyá _____.

wówičhak'u   p̄ȟóskil wičháyuze
wičháyužaža   čhašwíčhatȟuŋ
mniwíčhak'u

Ihíŋhaŋni yuŋkȟáŋ Lisa akhé čhúŋšoke-ta yé. Yuŋkȟáŋ šuŋȟpála eyá iyéwičhaye. Šuŋȟpála kiŋ líla záŋgzaŋkapi čha Lisa iwíčhačú na thiyáta awíčhakhi. Šuŋȟpála kiŋ líla šabšápapi čha Lisa _____. Šuŋȟpála kiŋ líla ločhíŋpi čha Lisa _____. Šuŋȟpála kiŋ líla ípuzapi čha Lisa _____. Lisa šuŋȟpála kiŋ líla waštéwičhalaka čha _____. Na heháŋl Lisa šuŋȟpála kiŋ iyóhila _____.

a Why is the affix **wičha** added to the verbs in the second paragraph? Do you remember? Circle the correct choice below.

- Because in the second paragraph she is talking about puppies that are not her own.
- Because in the second paragraph she is talking about more than one puppy.
- Because in the second paragraph she is talking about puppies that are female.

b Lisa is sending texts to her aunt about the puppies! Can you help her write the sentences she should send, like the examples? Remember, she will use the "I" form of the verb! Write on scrap paper.

Šuŋȟpála eyá iyéwičhawaye.
Šuŋȟpála kiŋ iwíčhawaču.
Šuŋȟpála kiŋ šabšápapi čha wičháblužaža.

30 Your teacher will give you a role play card. What you have done for the puppies is pictured on the card. Your partner will ask you what you have done. Answer according to what's on the card, like the model. Šuŋȟpála kiŋ lužáža he? -- Háŋ, blužáža / Hiyá, blužáža šni.

31 Work with a partner. Tell your partner one of the problems the puppies have, from the first set of choices. Your partner should suggest what the two of you should do to help, from the second set of choices.

> Šuŋȟpála kiŋ líla šabšápapi.
> Šuŋȟpála kiŋ líla ločhíŋpi.
> Šuŋȟpála kiŋ líla ípuzapi.
> Šuŋȟpála kiŋ iyókišičapi.
> Šuŋȟpála kiŋ watúkȟapi.

> Iyúŋg-wičhúŋkhiya héči.
> Wičhúŋyužaža héči.
> Wówičhuŋk'u héči.
> Pȟóskil wičhúŋyuza héči.
> Mniwíčhuŋk'u héči.

32 Look at the forms of the verb **yužáža** below. You will see forms for "I", "you" and "You and I". What happens when we combine **wičha** and **uŋ**?

Wičháblužaža. - I washed them.

Wičhálužaža. - You washed them.

Wičhúŋyužaža. - You and I washed them.

How do we write that combination?
Write the correct combination of **wičha** and **uŋ** here: _____.

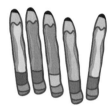

33 What do you do when you see a mark above "s" or "z"? How do you pronounce these letters? Let's practice!

a

sí, siŋté, snásna, sápe, sní, skúye, sóso, sagyé, sáŋ

b

šiná, šákpe, šašté, šlošló, šišóka, šiyóša, šlušlúte

č

zí, zizí, zičá, zaŋní, záptaŋ, zuzéča, zizípela, thezí

e

žiží, waŋží, žožó, tȟakóža, žaŋžáŋla, čhažé, yužúžu, uŋžíŋžiŋtka

Review Quiz

1 Can you pick the right form? Circle the correct choice in each pair.

1. Šuŋǧíla kiŋ lé hí skaská / skaskápi.
2. Šuŋǧíla kiŋ iyúha hí skaská / skaskápi.
3. Maštíŋčala kiŋ lé nakpá háŋskaska / háŋskaskapi.
4. Maštíŋčala kiŋ iyúha nakpá háŋskaska / háŋskaskapi.
5. Gnugnúška kiŋ lé ištá mimémela / mimémelapi.
6. Gnugnúška kiŋ iyúha ištá mimémela / mimémelapi.

2 Challenge! Do you know how to say these sentences in Lakota?

1. This horse is grazing.
2. Horses graze.
3. This eagle is flying.
4. Eagles fly.
5. This rabbit is jumping.
6. Rabbits jump.

3 What are horses like? How about robins? And trout? For each body part listed, write a sentence that tells what that body part is like in general for that animal.

Šúŋkawakȟáŋ

- hú: _____
- siŋté: _____
- híŋ: _____
- šuŋgsíšake: _____

Šišóka

- wíyaka: _____
- siŋtúpi: _____
- ȟupáhu: _____
- pȟasú: _____

Hoǧáŋwičhašašni

- ištá: _____
- hoápe: _____
- iyóȟa: _____
- hí: _____

4 Now can you write about Max, the horse? And Red, the robin? How about Speckle, the trout? How will your sentences change if you talk about a specific horse, instead of all horses in general? A specific robin? A specific trout? Write your sentences on scrap paper.

1 Iktómi, who always tries to fool people and animals, was roaming around the woods last night. Now, each animal is missing something! Iktómi took it! What did Iktómi take from each animal? Read what the animals say and draw lines to match the animal to the thing that Iktómi took from them.

Iktómi huhú waŋ imákiču.

Iktómi hoǧáŋ waŋ imákiču.

Iktómi čhaŋpȟá eyá imákiču.

Iktómi sú eyá imákiču.

Iktómi wítka eyá imákiču.

Iktómi makȟátomniča eyá imákiču.

2 Now let's pretend Iktómi showed up in your class! Sit in a circle. Your teacher will give each of you a card with an object on it. To start the game, one of you will pretend to be Iktómi. The rest of you will close your eyes. Iktómi will take something from someone in the group. When you open your eyes, if Iktómi took something from you, say so, like the model!

Itkó tȟaspáŋ waŋ imákiču.

3 **a** Pretend one of your brothers, sisters or cousins were playing, and accidentally damaged something of yours. Your teacher will give you a card with a picture of the thing that was damaged. This happened to your classmates too! Ask five of them what happened, like the model.

Táku tókȟa he?

Mitȟáŋkala haŋpóšpula waŋ makíyušiče.

b Now write a list of what everyone needs to replace at the store. Can you remember? Write sentences like the example for each of the people you talked with. Write them on scrap paper.

Mary thiblóku kiŋ haŋpóšpula waŋ kiyúšiče. Čha Mary haŋpóšpula waŋží opȟétȟuŋ kte.

4 **a** Now the animals are very sad because of the things Iktómi took from them. Iron Hawk, who always helps people in need, knows that the animals are sad. The animals ask Iron Hawk to get their things back for them. Can you help the animals finish their sentences? On a piece of scrap paper write a sentence for each animal about what he wants to get back, like the model.

Čhetáŋ Máza,_____kiŋ imákiču wo.

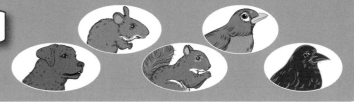

b When you have finished, your teacher will ask you to act out the conversations between Iron Hawk and each animal.

Čhatáŋ Máza sú kiŋ imákiču.

Oháŋ, héčhamuŋ kte!

5 **a** Iron Hawk has returned. Listen to the animals talking. Which of the animals did not get their things back? Circle the correct choices in the yellow bubbles.

mathó

huhú

kȟaŋǧí

zičá

itȟúŋkala

šišóka

Íčhiŋ Iktómi _____ kiŋ makíyušiče.

Íčhiŋ Iktómi _____ kiŋ tȟebmákhiye.

b Do you know why? Listen again. Then match the animal with the reason (in the green triangles) "why" Iron Hawk could not get their things back for them. For each sentence, write in the thing they didn't get back.

6 Abléza po!

a In the first picture, who is speaking?   **Bob   Mike**

   Who took the ball?   **Bob   Mike**

b In the second picture, who is speaking?   **Bob   Mike**

   Who took the ball?   **Bob   Mike**

č In which picture does Bob take the ball FROM Mike?   **1   2**

   In which picture does Bob take the ball FOR Mike?   **1   2**

Ečéš, tȟápa kiŋ imákiču!

1

Huŋhuŋhé, tȟápa kiŋ imákiču.

2

7 On the opposite page, there is the first part of a story about **Pȟehíŋ Žiží Wiŋ.** She finds several things at the bears' home. Skim through the first part of the story to see what she finds. Circle the words on the page and write three of them here:

a) _____ b) _____ č) _____

8 You have probably read a version of this story before! But now, let's read it in Lakota! Read the first paragraph and see if you can you answer all these questions in Lakota.

1. **Pȟehíŋ Žiží Wiŋ tuktél ománi he?**

   _____

2. **Pȟehíŋ Žiží Wiŋ táku waŋyáŋka he?**

   _____

3. **Pȟehíŋ Žiží Wiŋ táku él yá he?**

   _____

4. **Pȟehíŋ Žiží Wiŋ táku yuk'éȟk'eǧa he?**

   _____

5. **Ehákeȟčiŋ Pȟehíŋ Žiží Wiŋ táku tókȟuŋ he?**

   _____

9 Read the part of the story next to the second picture. Can you write what Pȟéhíŋ Žiží Wiŋ says about each bowl? Then, number the sentences in the order she says them.

☐ _____

1 _____ Wóžapi kiŋ lé líla eháš _____ kštó. _____

☐ _____

10 Read the same part of the story again. Can you figure out what "**iyútȟe**" means? Circle the best choice below:

to eat   to taste   to finish

Now check in the dictionary to see if you were right! Be careful, this is an ablaut verb! How do you spell it in the dictionary?

Pȟehíŋ Žiží Wiŋ Part 1

Toháŋtuka waŋ wičhíŋčala waŋ Pȟehíŋ Žiží Wiŋ ečíyapi. Aŋpétu waŋ él čhaŋmáhel ománi. Yuŋkȟáŋ thiíkčeya waŋ háŋ čha waŋyáŋka čhaŋkhé étkiya yé. Thiyópa kiŋ yuk'éȟk'eǧe, éyaš él tuwéni yaŋké šni, škȟá thimá iyáye.

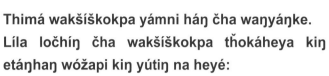

Thimá wakšíškokpa yámni háŋ čha waŋyáŋke. Líla ločhíŋ čha wakšíškokpa tȟokáheya kiŋ etáŋhaŋ wóžapi kiŋ yútiŋ na heyé:
"Ší, wóžapi kiŋ lé líla eháš kȟáte kštó," eyé.
Yuŋkȟáŋ wakšíškokpa ičínuŋpa kiŋ etáŋhaŋ wóžapi kiŋ yútiŋ na heyé:
"Ší, wóžapi kiŋ lé líla eháš sní kštó," eyé.
Heháŋl wakšíškokpa ičíyamni kiŋ etáŋhaŋ wóžapi kiŋ yútiŋ na heyé:
"Huŋhí, wóžapi kiŋ léš eyáš wahéhaŋyaŋ," iyúškiŋyaŋ eyíŋ na átaya tȟebyé.

Heháŋl líla ípuza čha takúŋl yatkíŋ kta olé. Yuŋkȟáŋ wíyatke yámni háŋ čha waŋyáŋke. Čhaŋkhé wíyatke kiŋ waŋží etáŋhaŋ yatkíŋ na heyé:
"Má! Waȟpé kiŋ lé líla eháš skúye kštó," eyé.
Ho čha wíyatke ičínuŋpa kiŋ etáŋhaŋ yatkíŋ na heyé:
"Má! Waȟpé kiŋ lé átayaš skúye šni kštó," eyé.
Ho čha ičíyamni kiŋ etáŋhaŋ yatkíŋ na heyé:
"Huŋhí, waȟpé kiŋ léš eyáš wahéhaŋyaŋ," eyíŋ na waȟpé kiŋ átaya yaȟépe.

Waŋná líla watúkȟa na ȟwá hiŋglé. Čhaŋkhé ptehíŋšma waŋ akáŋl iyúŋke, éyaš čhuwíta. Yuŋkȟáŋ šiná yámni waŋyáŋke. Ho čha šiná kiŋ waŋží ičú na aíglaȟpe. Yuŋkȟáŋ heyé:
"Má! Šiná kiŋ lé átayaš šóke ȟče šni," eyé.
Čhaŋkhé šiná ičínuŋpa kiŋ ičú na aíglaȟpe. Yuŋkȟáŋ heyé: "Má! Šiná kiŋ lé líla eháš šičámna kštó," eyé.
Čhaŋkhé šiná ičíyamni kiŋ ičú na aíglaȟpe. Yuŋkȟáŋ heyé: "Huŋhí, šiná kiŋ léš eyáš wahéhaŋyan," eyíŋ na waŋná haŋkéyaš očhósya ištíŋme.

11 **a** In the story Pȟehíŋ Žiží Wiŋ uses the words **eháš** and **eyáš**. Let's figure them out! Match the picture with the sentence. Look at the underlined words. Why do you think they are here?

1. Uŋzóǧe kiŋ lená eháš tȟáŋka.
2. Uŋzóǧe kiŋ lená eháš číkʼala.
3. Uŋzóǧe kiŋ lená eyáš wahéhaŋyaŋ.

b Now let's look at some other expressions used in the story. Read the sentences below, and pay attention to the blue highlighted expressions. Then, match each expression to the English expression that is closest in meaning.

Ógle kiŋ lé átaya šápe.

Ógle kiŋ lé átayaš šápe šni.

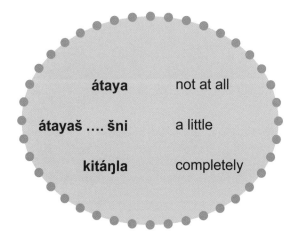

átaya	not at all
átayaš …. šni	a little
kitáŋla	completely

Ógle kiŋ lé kitáŋla šápe.

12 Go back to the story of Pȟehíŋ Žiží Wiŋ and read the part of the story matching the third picture. Can you answer the question below? Circle the correct choices.

a Táku čha olé he?
1. Takúŋl yútiŋ kta olé.
2. Takúŋl yatkíŋ kta olé.
3. Takúŋl akáŋ iyúŋkiŋ kta olé.

č Waȟpé ičínuŋpa kiŋ hé tákuwe waȟtélašni he?
1. Átayaš kȟáte šni čha hé uŋ.
2. Átayaš skúye šni čha hé uŋ.
3. Líla eháš sní čha hé uŋ.
4. Líla skúya čha hé uŋ.

b Waȟpé tȟokáhe kiŋ tákuwe waȟtélašni he?
1. Líla eháš kȟáta čha hé uŋ.
2. Líla eháš skúya čha hé uŋ.
3. Átayaš skúye šni čha hé uŋ.
4. Átayaš kȟáte šni čha hé uŋ.

e Waȟpé ičíyamni kiŋ hé tákuwe waštélaka he?
1. Átayaš wašté šni čha hé uŋ.
2. Eháš skúya čha hé uŋ.
3. Líla skúya čha hé uŋ.
4. Eyáš wahéčhetu čha hé uŋ.

13 In the story of Pȟehíŋ Žiží Wiŋ, read the part of the story next to the fourth picture. Can you answer the questions below? Circle the correct choices.

a Pȟehíŋ Žiží Wiŋ tákuwe šiná tȟokáheya kiŋ waȟtélašni he?

1. Šiná kiŋ hé líla eȟáš zibzípela čha hé uŋ.
2. Šiná kiŋ hé líla eȟáš ptéčela čha hé uŋ.
3. Šiná kiŋ hé líla eȟáš šičámna čha hé uŋ.
4. Šiná kiŋ hé líla eȟáš šá čha hé uŋ.

b Pȟehíŋ Žiží Wiŋ tákuwe šiná ičínuŋpa kiŋ waȟtélašni he?

1. Šiná kiŋ hé átayaš šóke šni čha hé uŋ.
2. Šiná kiŋ hé líla eȟáš šóke čha hé uŋ.
3. Šiná kiŋ hé líla eȟáš šičámna čha hé uŋ.
4. Šiná kiŋ hé líla eȟáš ptéčela čha hé uŋ.

č Pȟehíŋ Žiží Wiŋ tákuwe šiná ičíyamni kiŋ waštélaka he?

1. Šiná kiŋ hé líla eȟáš tȟáŋka čha hé uŋ.
2. Šiná kiŋ hé eyáš waȟéčhetu čha hé uŋ.
3. Šiná kiŋ hé átayaš háŋske šni čha hé uŋ.
4. Šiná kiŋ hé átayaš šóke šni hé uŋ.

14 # Abléza po!

How do we tell when Pȟehíŋ Žiží Wiŋ was speaking in the story?
What word was always used before her sentence? Write it here: _____
What word was always used after her sentence? Write it here: _____

Waȟpé kiŋ lé eyáš waȟéčhetu.

Pȟehíŋ Žiží Wiŋ heyé: "Waȟpé kiŋ lé eyáš waȟéčhetu," eyé.

15 Okay, let's try to use **heyé** and **eyé**! Kimi was not in school Monday, so Lisa is writing her an email about what everyone said they did over the weekend. Can you help Lisa finish her email? Write the sentences on a piece of scratch paper, like the model below.

Ȟtálehaŋ walówaŋ.

Ȟtálehaŋ kiŋyékhiyapi waŋ wakáǧe.

Wačhípi waŋ ektá waí.

Ȟtálehaŋ uŋčí waŋglág waí.

Ȟtálehaŋ tȟabwáškate ló.

Ȟtálehaŋ wawákšu.

Bob heyé, "Ȟtálehaŋ walówaŋ." eyé.

16 Now, let's get back to our story! When the bears come home, they notice that some of their things are not they way they left them. Skim through the part of this story on this page and write the Lakota names of those things here:

a) _____ b) _____ č) _____

Pȟehíŋ Žiží Wiŋ Part 2

Ištíŋme ečhúŋhaŋ Matȟó yámni kiŋ thiyáta glípi.
Yuŋkȟáŋ matȟó bloká kiŋ wakšíškokpa kiŋ waŋglákiŋ na heyé:

"Hóȟ, tuwá wóžapi kiŋ makíyute ló," eyé.

Ho na matȟó wíŋyela kiŋ wakšíškokpa kiŋ waŋglákiŋ na heyé:

"Ečéš tuwá wóžapi kiŋ makíyute kštó," eyé.

Ho na matȟó čhiŋčála kiŋ wakšíškokpa kiŋ waŋglákiŋ na heyé:

"Hóȟ, tuwá wóžapi kiŋ tȟebmákhiye ló," eyé.

Hehánl matȟó bloká kiŋ wíyatke kiŋ waŋglákiŋ na heyé:

"Hóȟ, tuwá waȟpé kiŋ makíyatke ló," eyé.

Ho na matȟó wíŋyela kiŋ wíyatke kiŋ waŋglákiŋ na heyé:

"Ečéš tuwá waȟpé kiŋ makíyatke kštó," eyé.

Ho na matȟó čhiŋčála kiŋ wíyatke kiŋ waŋglákiŋ na heyé:

"Hóȟ, tuwá waȟpé kiŋ átaya makíyaȟepe ló," eyá čhéya škhé.

Yuŋkȟáŋ matȟó bloká kiŋ šiná kiŋ waŋglákiŋ na heyé:

"Hóȟ, tuwá šiná kiŋ imákiču weló," eyá škhé.
Hehánl matȟó wíŋyela kiŋ šiná kiŋ waŋglákiŋ na heyé:

"Ečéš tuwá šiná kiŋ imákiču kštó," eyá škhé.
Hehánl matȟó čhiŋčála kiŋ Pȟehíŋ Žiží Wiŋ waŋyáŋkiŋ na heyé:

"Hóȟ, tuwá šiná kiŋ imákiču na héčhena makíuŋ weló," eyá čhéya škhé.

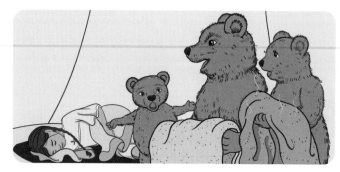

Yuŋkȟáŋ Pȟehíŋ Žiží Wiŋ kiktá hiyáyiŋ na matȟó yámni kiŋ waŋwíčhayaŋke.
Ho čha "Hoští," eyíŋ na tȟaŋkátakiya napȟá škhé.

Thiyópa kiŋ yuğáŋ na čhaŋyátakiya íŋyaŋgyaŋ yé. Matȟó yámni thípi kiŋ él ičínuŋpani yé šni čhaŋkhé akhé waŋyáŋkapi šni.

17 Read through the first paragraph of part 2. First, can you match each bowl with the correct bear? Next, can you write the correct verb next to each bowl, using the verbs from the story?

18 Next, draw lines to match the bears with their cups.

19 Now, draw lines to match the bears with their blankets.

20 Read the fourth paragraph. First, can you number the pictures below in the correct order? Next, write the verb that matches each picture in the blank beneath the picture.

ištíŋme

waŋwíčhayaŋke

napȟé

_____ _____ _____

21 Read through the last paragraph of the story again, and answer the following questions. Circle the correct answer.

a Táku čha yuǧáŋ he?

- Čhaŋóphiye waŋ.
- Thiyópa waŋ.
- Ožáŋžaŋglepi waŋ.

b Pȟehíŋ Žiží Wiŋ tókhetkiya íŋyaŋka he?

- thiyátakiya
- wakpátakiya
- čhaŋyátakiya
- otȟúŋwahetakiya

č Pȟehíŋ Žiží Wiŋ ičínuŋpa Matȟó Yámni thípi kiŋ ektá yá he?

Háŋ / Hiyá

e Matȟó yámni kiŋ Pȟehíŋ Žiží Wiŋ ičínuŋpa waŋyáŋkapi he?

Háŋ / Hiyá

131

22 **a** In the story, can you find the verbs that the bears use when complaining about what Pȟehíŋ Žiží Wiŋ has done to their things? Turn back to page 130 and circle them in the story!

b Write those verbs in the column on the left below.
Then, draw lines to match those verbs with the dictionary forms on the right.

makíyušíče

_____

_____

_____

_____

_____

tȟebkhíye

ikíču

kiyáȟepe

kiyátke

kiyúte

kiyúšiče

23 Abléza po!

Look at the sentence diagram below and answer the questions.

1. Whose cup of tea is this? Write it here: _____
2. Who is drinking the tea? Write it here: _____

Pȟehíŋ Žiží Wiŋ matȟó wíŋyela kiŋ waȟpé kiŋ **kiyátke.**

24 Now, can you write a sentence about each thing that happened? Write the story yourself (nine sentences) on a piece of scrap paper, like the model.

Pȟehíŋ Žiží Wiŋ matȟó čhiŋčála kiŋ šiná kiŋ ikíču.

25 Now let's figure out the difference between **ičú** and **ikíču**! Let's look at this example: Mike and Tȟašína find some plums when they come back to their classroom after gym. Look at the pictures below, and circle all the correct answers for each question.

> Wáŋ ká wáŋ, kȟáŋta yámni. Kaná tuwá tȟáwa he?

> Kaná tuwá tȟáwa héči slolwáye šni, k'éyaš waŋží iwáču kte kštó.

> Míš-eyá waŋží iwáču kte ló. Paŋȟyá lowáčhiŋ.

> Hóȟ, tuwá kȟáŋta núŋm imákiču!

a Tuwá kȟáŋta kiŋ waŋží ičú he?

-- Mike kȟáŋta waŋ ičú.
-- Tȟašína kȟáŋta waŋ ičú.
-- Tuwéni kȟáŋta waŋžíni ičú šni.

b Kȟáŋta kiŋ kaná tuwá tȟáwa he?

-- Mike tȟáwa.
-- Tȟašína tȟáwa.
-- Slol'úŋyaŋpi šni.

č Kȟáŋta k'uŋ hená tuwá tȟáwa héči slolyáya he?

-- Kȟáŋta kiŋ Mike tȟáwa.
-- Kȟáŋta kiŋ Tȟašína tȟáwa.
-- Kȟáŋta kiŋ Bob tȟáwa.

e Tuwá Bob kȟáŋta kiŋ ikíču he?

- Mike Bob kȟáŋta waŋ ikíču.
- Tȟašína Bob kȟáŋta waŋ ikíču.
- Summer Bob kȟáŋta waŋ ikíču.

26 Abléza po!

a Why do we say **ikíču** instead of **ičú** in the second picture? Circle the correct answer.

- because they were Mike's own plums.
- because they did not belong to anyone.
- because they belonged to Bob but Mike and Tȟašína took the plums from him.

b What affix is used in this example to indicate that the plums were taken from Bob? Circle the correct answer.

wa-   uŋ-

ya-   ki-

27 a Sit in a circle. Your teacher will tell one of you to take a piece of candy, like this: "**Waskúyeča waŋží ičú wo/we.**" Now, choose someone in the circle and give them the same command!

b Next, your teacher will select one of you to pretend to be the trickster Iktómi. The rest of the class will close their eyes, and you take the candy from someone! When everyone opens their eyes again, the person whose candy is missing should say: "**Iktómi waskúyeča kiŋ imákiču.**"

č Now write an email about what happened. What did Iktómi do in your classroom? Here is an idea to model your sentences after. Write three or four sentences.

Itkómi Patti waskúyeča waŋ ikiču.

28 The teacher tells the students they can come and take a piece of candy from her desk, but Kimi is busy working on her art project! What does she ask Matȟó? Read the conversation and answer the question by circling the correct answer.

> Oháŋ, waŋží ičhíčiču kte. Oówa kiŋ tukté waŋží yačhíŋ he?

> Omákȟaŋ šni, waskúyeča waŋží imákiču we.

> Šá waŋží imákiču we.

What does Kimi ask Matȟó to do?

- To eat her candy.
- To take a candy.
- To take a candy for her.
- To do her work.

29 Abléza po!

a Which affix do we use in this case to show that Matȟó is taking something **for** Kimi? Circle it.

wa-   **ya-**   **ki-**   **uŋ-**

b Is it the same affix that we used to show that Iktómi was taking something **from** the animals?

Yes   No

30 Your teacher has new pens, paper and books on his or her desk! Pretend that you need one of these things, but you are busy doing something. Ask someone in your class to take a pen, a piece of paper, or a book for you, like the model:

Wíčazo waŋží imákičhu nitȟó.

Ohaŋ, waŋží ičhíčičhu kte.

Waŋ lé waŋ, lé ičhíčičhu.

Philámayaye kštó.

31 Let's play a guessing game! Work with a partner in the circle. Your teacher will give you pictures of things and animals. Show one of them to your partner, but don't let anyone else know which picture you showed. The others in the circle have to guess by asking questions, like the models.

Matȟó waŋží ničípazo he?

Šúŋka waŋží ničípazo he?

Hiyá, matȟó waŋžíni makípazo šni.

Háŋ, šúŋka waŋ makípazo.

32 ⓐ One of your classmates is coming to visit you tomorrow! What will you show them of yours? Make a list in Lakota of what you will show him/her on a piece of scrap paper.

ⓑ Answer your friends' questions, like the model:

Híŋhaŋni kiŋ waŋčhíyaŋg waú kte. Táku čha mayákipazo kta he?

Iyéčhiŋkyaŋke waŋ čhičípazo kte.

č̌ Now, draw pictures of what your friends are going to show you. Show the pictures to the friends you talked with. Did you draw the right things?

Wóuŋspe 10

33 Can you fill in the speech bubbles? What happened to each of the children? Use the vocabulary from the Pȟehíŋ Žiží Wiŋ story to help you.

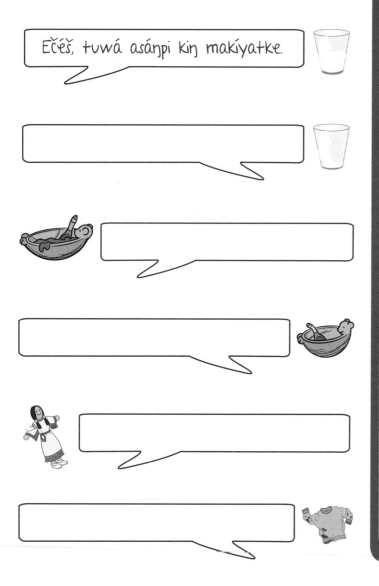

Ečéš, tuwá asáŋpi kiŋ makíyatke.

34 Abléza po!

a Can you match the verb forms on the left with the root forms of the verbs on the right? Draw lines to match.

kiyútA	yušíčA
kaú	yútA
kiyátkAŋ	mas'ápȟA
kíčaǧA	ičú
kiyáȟepA	opȟétȟuŋ
tȟebkhíyA	pazó
ikíču	káǧA
mas'ákipȟA	úŋ
opȟékičatȟuŋ	yaȟépA
kipázo	aú
kiyúšičA	tȟebyÁ
kiúŋ	yatkÁŋ

b Now, can you figure out what the affix is in the verbs on the left? For each verb, underline the affix.

č Next, make a list of the affixes that are used to say that something is done **to** someone or **for** someone. (Hint: There are four!).

35 Let's do a quick review! Do you remember the verbs that talk about doing something **with** your own things? How do those verbs look different from the verbs we are doing now, that talk about doing something **to** or **for** someone else?

Look at the sentences to the right. Circle the sentences that talk about doing something **with** your own things. Underline the sentences that talk about doing something **to** or **for** someone else.

1. Waskúyeča waŋ ikíkču.
2. Waskúyeča waŋ ikíču.
3. Wóžapi kiŋ tȟebkíye.
4. Wóžapi kiŋ tȟebkhíye.
5. Asáŋpi kiŋ glatkáŋ.
6. Asáŋpi kiŋ kiyátkaŋ.
7. Wówapi kiŋ gluǧáŋ.
8. Bloókpaŋla kiŋ kiyúǧaŋ.
9. Aǧúyapi kiŋ glúte.
10. Aǧúyapi kiŋ kiyúte.

36 The children went to the Black Hills for an overnight trip! Now they are getting ready to come home, and they are trying to sort out their things. Look at the pictures below, then skim through the children's conversation. Circle the items they talk about.

Lisa: Summer, ógle zigzíča kiŋ imáyakiču kštó.

Summer: Hiyá, ógle zigzíča kiŋ ičhíčiču šni. Mitȟáwa kiŋ iwékču kštó! Nitȟáwa kiŋ héčhena wičhášitȟokšu imáhel úŋ.

Tȟašína: Ečéš tuwá mní kiŋ átaya makíyaȟepe. Mike, mní kiŋ mayákiyaȟepe, iŋčhéye?

Mike: Hiyá, mní kiŋ čhičíyaȟepe šni yeló. Mitȟáwa kiŋ wagláȟepe. Matȟó nitȟáwa kiŋ ničíyaȟepe. Na nakúŋ líla áiniȟaťe!

Tȟašína: Íŋska, Matȟó aǧúyapi kiŋ tȟebwákhiye! Líla lowáčhiŋ na wóyute maníče.

Matȟó: Haúŋ, tuwá bloókpaŋla kiŋ makíyuǧaŋ. Summer, bloókpaŋla kiŋ mayákiyuǧaŋ he?

Summer: Hiyá, čhičíyuǧaŋ šni. Míš bloókpaŋla kiŋ waglúǧaŋ. Lisa šúŋka tȟáwa kiŋ ničíyuǧaŋ kštó.

37 Read back through the children's conversations, and then decide whether the following sentences are true or false. Hint: remember the difference between verbs that talk about doing something **with** your own things, and doing something **to** or **for** somebody else.

1. Summer Lisa ógle zigzíča kiŋ ikíču. Háŋ / Hiyá
2. Summer ógle zigzíča kiŋ ikíkču. Háŋ / Hiyá
3. Lisa Summer ógle zigzíča kiŋ ikíču. Háŋ / Hiyá
4. Tȟašína mní kiŋ glaȟépe. Háŋ / Hiyá
5. Tȟašína Mike mní kiŋ kiyáȟepe. Háŋ / Hiyá
6. Mike Tȟašína mní kiŋ kiyáȟepe. Háŋ / Hiyá
7. Matȟó aǧúyapi kiŋ tȟebkíye. Háŋ / Hiyá
8. Matȟó Tȟašína aǧúyapi kiŋ tȟebkíye. Háŋ / Hiyá
9. Tȟašína Matȟó aǧúyapi kiŋ tȟebkhíye. Háŋ / Hiyá
10. Matȟó bloókpaŋla kiŋ gluǧáŋ. Háŋ / Hiyá
11. Summer Matȟó bloókpaŋla kiŋ kiyúǧaŋ. Háŋ / Hiyá
12. Summer bloókpaŋla kiŋ gluǧáŋ. Háŋ / Hiyá

38 Now it's your turn! Choose one of the three sets of words, and write your own story! Did the blackbirds eat their own berries? Did another animal come and eat their berries? It's up to you! When you have finished, read your story to the class. Your classmates should act out what happened in your story.

1

watȟókeča
wáblošá
šuŋǧíla
tȟebkhíyA
tȟebkíyA
glaȟépA
kiyáȟepA

2

kȟaŋǧí
waŋblí
hoȟpí
čhaŋwápe
ikíču
ikíkču
glušíčA
kiyúšičA

3

pispíza
pȟehíŋ
waȟpé
mní
glútA
kiyútA
glatkÁŋ
kiyátkAŋ

39

Which form should we use? Circle the correct choice of the two possibilities in parentheses. In the sentence, the object belongs to the person who is encircled with it.

a Bob (Matȟó agúyapi) waŋ (glúte / kiyúte).

e (Summer haŋpóšpula) waŋ (glušíče / kiyúšiče).

b Lisa (Tȟašína čhaŋkȟóžuha) kiŋ lé (kpazó / kipázo).

g Tȟašína (Kimi tȟaspáŋ haŋpí) waŋ (yaȟépe / kiyáȟepe).

č (Matȟó mnikápȟopapi) kiŋ lé (glatké / kiyátke).

ǧ Mike (James agúyapi) waŋ (tȟebkíye / tȟebkhíye).

40

Show how much you know! Fill in the missing parts of the chart.

I	•	wówak'u	•	waí	•		•	waȟtéwalašni	•	
you (singular)	•	wóyak'u	•		•		•		•	
he/she/it	•	wók'u	•		•		•		•	olé
you and I	•	wóuŋk'u	•		•		•	waȟtéuŋlapišni	•	
we	•	wóuŋk'upi	•		•	uŋkápȟepi	•		•	
you (plural)	•	wóyak'upi	•		•		•		•	
they	•	wók'upi	•		•	apȟépi	•		•	

I	•	blužáža	•	waŋbláke	•		•		•	ibláble
you (singular)	•	lužáža	•		•	oláke	•	ílotake	•	
he/she/it	•	yužáža	•		•		•		•	
you and I	•	uŋyúžaža	•		•		•	uŋkíyotake	•	
we	•	uŋyúžažapi	•		•		•		•	
you (plural)	•	lužážapi	•		•		•		•	
they	•	yužážapi	•	waŋyáŋkapi	•		•		•	

I	•	wamátukȟa	•		•	uŋmáspe	•		•	húmastake
you (singular)	•	wanítukȟa	•		•		•	ničhúwita	•	
he/she/it	•	watúkȟa	•	okȟáte	•		•		•	
you and I	•	waúŋtukȟa	•		•		•	čhuwíta	•	
we	•	waúŋtukȟapi	•		•	uŋkúŋspepi	•		•	
you (plural)	•	wanítukȟapi	•	oníkȟatapi	•		•		•	
they	•	watúkȟapi	•		•		•		•	hústakapi

Review Quiz

1 Some of the children are playing tricks on the others! They are taking each other's things! Can you fill in the speech bubbles for each child, following the pictures, like the model?

Lisa tȟaspáŋ waŋ imákičų!

2 Challenge! Can you say these sentences in Lakota?

a. He took my doll from me!

_____

b. Take an apple for me!

_____

č. Tȟašína damaged my phone!

_____

e. Mike ate up my sandwich (on me)!

_____

g. Bob opened my potato chips (on me)!

_____

ǧ. Summer took a pop for Lisa.

_____

3 Put the words of these sentences in the correct together.

a. tȟápa waŋ / ikíču. / atkúku kiŋ / Bob

_____

b. tȟaŋkáku / lé / Summer / kiyúšiče. / haŋpóšpula kiŋ

_____

č. kiyáȟepe. / Tȟašína / mnikápȟopapi kiŋ / čépȟaŋšitku / lé

_____

e. Challenge!
Bob / waŋží opȟétȟuŋ / kiŋyékhiyapi kiŋ / lé / Bob kiŋyékhiyapi / kte. / suŋkáku / kiyúšiče čha

_____

4 Can you rewrite what each child says in the speech bubbles, to tell Lisa what happened in an email? Do you remember what words you need to add before and after the direct speech?

Kimi aǧúyapi kiŋ lé tȟebmákhiye!

_____

Summer čhuwígnaka waŋ makípazo!

_____

Mike tȟaspáŋ waŋ tȟebmákhiye!

_____

James wówapi kiŋ lé imákiču!

Glossary

aglágla - alongside smth; (pg 110, 111)

ačháŋzekA - to be angry with sb; (pg 6, 9)

ačhípȟe → apȟé; (pg 38)

aǧúyapi - bread; (pg 137)

aǧúyapi aǧúǧu - toast; (pg 51)

aǧúyapi oštéka - taco; (pg 80)

ahíyokas'iŋ - to peek in/out this way; (pg 108)

akhé - again; (pg 80, 82,121, 130)

akhí - to take smth back there; (pg 28, 121)

akáŋ / akáŋl - on; (pg 32, 42, 60, 95, 111, 127, 128)

akáŋlkaŋl - on in each case; (pg 113)

akáŋmaŋke → akáŋyaŋkA; (pg 13)

akáŋyaŋkA - to ride on (as on a horse); (pg 13)

akézaptaŋ - fifteen; (pg 32, 78)

akísni - to calm down, to stop (as rain); to recover from; (pg 85)

akíčhiyapi - contest; (pg 58)

akíȟ'aŋmat'e → akíȟ'aŋt'A; (pg 100)

akíȟ'aŋnit'e → akíȟ'aŋt'A; (pg 100)

akíȟ'aŋnič'iyiŋ → akíȟ'aŋič'iyA; (pg 42)

akíȟ'aŋič'iyA - to fast; (pg 42)

akíȟ'aŋt'A - to laugh at sb; (pg 100)

alí - to climb on smth; (pg 110, 113, 120)

alúpte → ayúptA; (pg 36)

alúta → ayúta; (pg 36)

alúštaŋ → ayúštaŋ; (pg 36)

amápȟe → apȟÁ; (pg 6)

amáyapȟa → apȟÁ; (pg 38)

amáyuštaŋ → ayúštaŋ; (pg 37)

amáčhaŋzeke → ačháŋzekA; (pg 6)

anáuŋǧoptaŋ → anáǧoptaŋ; (pg 85)

anáǧoptaŋ - to turn one's ear to smth/sb, to listen to; (pg 85)

aŋpétu - (pg 29, 94, 113, 120, 127)

apsíčA - to jump on or over smth; (pg 28)

apé - insect's wing; (pg 105)

apȟé 1 → apȟÁ; (pg 32, 37, 38)

apȟé 2 - to wait for sb

apȟÁ - to hit sb; (pg 37, 38)

apȟéyohaŋ - a horse's mane; (pg 12, 102)

asáŋpi - milk; (pg 136)

aškíyuwi - braid bands; (pg 53)

até - my father; (pg 19)

átaya - completely, entirely; (pg 111, 127, 128)

átayaš - completely, entirely; (pg 127, 128)

awápȟe → apȟÁ; (pg 38)

awáŋlake → awáŋyaŋkA; (pg 36)

awáŋyaŋkA - to look after smth/sb; (pg 41)

awáštelakA - to like or enjoy doing smth; (pg 62, 67,117)

awáštewalake → awáštelakA; (pg 62, 66, 67)

awášteyalake → awáštelakA; (pg 67)

awíčhakhi → akhí; (pg 121)

ayápȟe-ȟča → apȟÁ; (pg 38)

ayúptA - to answer smth/sb; (pg 36)

ayúta - to glance at smth/sb; (pg 9, 11, 22, 26, 36, 37, 57)

ayúštaŋ - to leave smth/sb, to let alone; (pg 36, 37)

azílyA - to smudge or cleanse smth/sb with herb smoke; (pg 43, 94)

aíglaȟpA - to cover oneself; (pg 127)

aímaȟat'e → aíȟat'A; (pg 7, 8, 9, 22)

aíniȟat'e! → aíȟat'A; (pg 137)

aíwaȟat'e → aíȟat'A; (pg 60, 137)

aíȟat'A - to laugh at sb; (pg 6, 38,137)

aóhomni(yaŋ) - around smth; (pg 82)

átaš - entirely, completely; (pg 25)

aú - to be bringing smth/sb here; (pg 136)

aúŋ - to put smth (as wood) on fire; (pg 41)

blawá → yawá; (pg 62)

blé 1 → yÁ; (pg 76)

blé 2 - lake

blihíč'iyA - to take courage, to hang in there; (pg 43)

bló - potatoes; (pg 80)

blokétu - it is summer; (pg 62, 63,68, 111, 117)

bloókpaŋla - potato chips; (pg 34, 136, 137)

blušlá → yušlá; (pg 43)

bluȟíče → yuȟíčA; (pg 38)

čépȟaŋši - my female cousin (female speaking); (pg 44)

čha - so, and so; (pg 56)

čha hé uŋ - that is why; (pg 120, 128, 129)

čháŋ - wood, tree, stick; (pg 41, 88, 94)

čhaŋáletka - tree branch; (pg 88)

čhaŋ-álipi - to climb up a tree; (pg 113)

čhaŋáuŋpi - fuel wood; (pg 94)

čhaŋhá - tree bark; (pg 88, 89, 90, 117)

čhaŋhá mahétaŋhaŋ - inner bark of a tree; (pg 117)

čhaŋháŋpi - sugar; (pg 94)

čhaŋhútkȟaŋ - tree roots; (pg 88)

čhaŋíwakse - a saw; (pg 41)

čhaŋkábu - to play the drum; (pg 39, 71)

čhaŋkhé - so, and so, therefore; (pg 24, 25, 43, 58, 94, 95)

čhaŋkȟóžuha - flint bag, strike-a-light pouch; (pg 53)

čhaŋkú - road, path; (pg 82, 110, 111)

čhaŋlí - tobacco; (pg 40, 94)

čhaŋmáhel - in the woods; (pg 44, 95, 127)

čhaŋmháŋska - candy; (pg 80)

čháŋna - whenever … then; (pg 6, 13, 23, 60, 62, 63, 68, 89, 94, 111, 113, 117, 120)

čhaŋnúŋpa - a pipe; (pg 42, 94)

čhaŋókpaŋ - wood chips, kindling; (pg 41, 42)

čhaŋóphiye - a wooden box; (pg 59, 60, 131)

čhaŋpȟá - chokecherry; (pg 124)

čhaŋsákala - a twig, switch; (pg 88, 92, 93, 94, 95, 117, 118)

čhaŋšáša - red osier dogwood; (pg 89, 94)

čhaŋšíŋ - resin; (pg 88, 118)

čháŋ-šna - when … usually then; (pg 13)

čhaŋšúška - box elder; (pg 90, 94)

čháŋwak'iŋ - saddle; (pg 11)

čháŋwak'iŋ iyákaškA - to put a saddle on a horse; (pg 12)

čháŋwak'iŋ khí - to take a saddle off a horse; (pg 12)

čhaŋwákabu → čhaŋkábu; (pg 62, 71)

čhaŋwákšiča - wooden bowl; (pg 94)

čhaŋwáŋkal - up on a tree; (pg 110, 111)

čhaŋwápe (wahpé) - tree leaf; (pg 88, 89)

čhaŋyáta - in the woods; (pg 28, 95, 130, 131)

čhaŋyátakiya - into the woods; (pg 28,130, 131)

čhaŋzékA - to be angry; (pg 99)

čhap'óle - to hunt beavers; (pg 108)

čhápa - beaver; (pg 44, 111, 117)

čhaštȟúŋ - to name sb/smth; (pg 121)

čhašwíčhathuŋ → čhaštȟúŋ; (pg 121)

čhatkáyatakiya - to the left; (pg 81, 82)

čhažé - someone's name; (pg 22, 69, 122)

čhéǧa - a pot, bucket; (pg 12. 41)

čhegnáke - breechcloth, loin cloth; (pg 52)

čhehňáǧa - soot, dead coals; (pg 41)

čhépA - to be fat; (pg 44, 99)

čhethí - to make fire; (pg 39, 41, 43, 70)

čhéyA - to cry; (pg 60, 130)

čheží - his/her tongue; (pg 104, 105)

čhič'ú → k'ú (pg 32, 33, 34, 95)

čhičhí - I took it from you, → khí; (pg 44)

čhičípazo → kipázo; (pg 135)

čhičíyaȟepe → kiyáȟepA; (pg 137)

čhičíyuǧaŋ → kiyúǧaŋ; (pg 137)

čhíŋ - to want smth; (pg 32, 80)

čhiŋčála - a young of an animal; (pg 31, 113, 118, 130)

čhíŋkpa - tree buds; (pg 88, 117, 118)

čhíŋkš - my son (term of address); (pg 46)

čhiyéku - his older brother; (pg 32, 43)

čhiyúȟiče → yuȟíčA; (pg 38)

čhó - cool; (pg 44); U9(pg 110)

čhóla - without; (pg 44, 48, 59)

čhoȟwáŋžiča - sandbar willow; (pg 90, 94)

čhúŋkš - my daughter (term of address); (pg 46, 47)

čhúŋšoke - woods, forest; (pg 121)

čhuwígnaka - a dress; (pg 3, 6, 44, 48, 139)

čhuwíta - to feel cold; (pg 44, 99, 100, 120, 127)

čičí - a boogyman; (pg 44)

čík'ala - to be small; (pg 44), (pg 116)

čikčík'ala → čík'ala; (pg 13, 44, 116, 112)

čísčila - to be small; (pg 44)

é - to be (identification of a specific person or thing); (pg 6, 8, 13, 80)

ečéš - Oh, gee, no! (disapproval, doubt, disbelief); (pg 125, 130, 136, 137)

ečháŋmi → ečhíŋ; (pg 80, 111)

ečhétkiya - in the direction of smth/sb; (pg 80, 111)

Glossary

ečhíŋ - to think that (follows a quote); (pg 94, 95)

ečhúŋhaŋ - in the meantime, at the same time; (pg 130)

ečíyapi - to be called; (pg 32, 127)

éeye - instead; (pg 32)

égnakA - to lay smth/sb down; (pg 19, 41, 79)

ehákeȟčiŋ - lastly; (pg 41 81, 119, 126)

eháŋuŋ - Aha! Indeed!; (pg 13, 100, 111, 119)

eháš - too much; (pg 95, 127, 128, 129)

ektá - at, to, in; (pg 35, 98, 110)

él - in, at; (pg 14, 29, 43)

enána - sometimes, occasionally; (pg 62, 63)

éoyakA - to go and tell or report smth; (pg 112)

epȟé → **eyÁ**; (pg 80, 96, 99)

etáŋ - some, any (17, 33, 34, 40, 41, 42, 45, 60, 64, 80, 85, 94, 95, 98, 100, 109)

etáŋhaŋ – from, out of (127)

éthi - to go there and make camp (pg 70)

étkiya - toward, at, in the direction of ; (pg 127)

éwektuŋže - to forget about sth, sb; (pg 47, 48, 49)

eyÁ - to say smth; (pg 3, 20, 27, 34, 37, 43, 60, 80, 94, 95, 121, 124, 130)

éyaš - but

eyáš - sufficient, enough, that will do

eyášna - usually; (pg 13, 62, 118)

eyíŋ → **eyÁ**; (pg 127, 130)

glaȟépA - to drink one's own up; (pg 137)

glatkÁŋ - to drink one's own; (pg 49, 54, 136)

glí - to come back;

gluǧáŋ - to open one's own; (pg 50, 54)

gluhá - to have one's own; (pg 49, 60)

glušíčA - to damage one's own; (pg 137)

glušlókA - to pull one's own off; (pg 59)

glútA - to eat one's own; (pg 49, 56, 137)

glužáža - to wash one's own; (pg 49, 59)

gmigmégmela → **gmigméla**; (pg 89)

gmigméla - to be round; (pg 91, 92, 112)

gmúŋkA - to trap smth/sb, catch in a trap; (pg 23)

gnašká - frog; (pg 104, 117)

gnugnúška - grasshopper; (pg 95, 118)

gnúni - to lose smth; (pg 58, 60)

ǧáŋ - to have messy or unkempt hair; (pg 51)

ǧí - to be brown; (pg 51)

ǧiǧípi → **ǧí**; (pg 112)

ǧópA - to snore; (pg 51)

ǧú - to be burned on the surface; (pg 11, 51)

haípažaža - soap; (pg 100)

hakíč'uŋ - to get dressed; (pg 60)

haŋbléčheyA - to cry for a vision, go on a vision quest; (pg 32, 43)

haŋhépi - it is night; (pg 32, 111, 113, 120)

haŋkéyaš - finally, at last; (pg 127)

haŋp'íkčeka - moccasins; (pg 108)

háŋpa - shoes; (pg 4, 29, 47, 54)

haŋpíkčeka - moccasins; (pg 33, 48, 54, 58, 59, 60)

haŋpóšpula - doll; (pg 3, 6, 47, 124)

háŋskA - to be long or tall; (pg 10, 58, 91, 97)

háŋskaska → **háŋskA**; (pg 89, 90, 91)

háŋtaŋš - if; (pg 99)

haótkeye - closet; (pg 59)

hayápi - clothes; (pg 63)

hé - that near the listener

hé - horn; (pg 102, 105)

he? - question ending

heȟáka - elk; (pg 36, 102, 114)

héčhamuŋ → **héčhuŋ**; (pg 125)

héčha - to be of such kind; (pg 10, 42, 44, 80,93, 117, 98)

héčhena - still; (pg 27, 130, 137)

hečhíŋ - to think that (before a quote); (pg 94, 95)

héčhiya - there; (pg 32, 43, 80)

héčhuŋ - to do that; (pg 110)

héči - marks a polite suggestion; (pg 44, 74, 80, 111, 118, 122, 133)

héhaŋ - at that time, back then; (pg 14, 58, 60, 78)

heháŋl - next, then, after that; (pg 41, 42, 43, 59, 80, 81, 95, 119, 121, 127, 130)

heháŋyaŋ - for that long or far; (pg 78)

hemáčha → **héčha**; (pg 36, 62, 102, 103, 104, 108)

hená - those near the listener; (pg 10, 29, 80, 95, 118, 133) henícha → **héčha**; (pg 102, 103, 106)

hepȟé → **heyÁ**; (pg 80)

hetáŋhaŋ - from there; (pg 81)

heúŋčha → **héčha**; (pg 119)

heyÁ - to say that

heyé: "___," eyé - "___," - he/she said; (pg 8, 37, 59, 80, 94, 95, 101, 127, 129, 130)

hí - to come; (pg 4, 5, 8, 17)

hí - tooth, teeth; (pg 102, 104, 105, 106, 115)

hiípažaža - toothbrush; (pg 49)

híŋ - fur, body hair; (pg 30, 80, 102, 103, 105, 112, 116)

hiŋglÁ - it happened or became suddenly

hiŋháŋ - owl; (pg 29, 37,117)

híŋhaŋni - it is morning; (pg 3, 29, 80, 98, 135)

hiŋíkčeka - dark bay horse, dark brown horse; (pg 13)

híŋȟota - gray horse; (pg 13)

híŋša - sorrel horse; (pg 13)

hiŋšmÁ - to be furry

hiŋšmášmapi → **hiŋšmÁ**; (pg 112)

híŋtȟo - gray horse; (pg 13)

híŋzi - buckskin horse; (pg 13)

hitȟúŋka - a rodent; (pg 117)

hiyáyiŋ → **kiktá hiyáyA**; (pg 130)

hiyúkiyA - to send one's own forward, → **pathíma**; (pg 101)

hóȟ - male expression of denial or doubt; (pg 103, 130, 133)

ho - well; (pg 14, 41, 43, 45, 62, 80, 85, 95, 127, 130)

hoápe - fish fins; (pg 105)

hoǧáŋ - fish; (pg 105, 114, 124)

hoíčhuwa - fishing tackle; (pg 18, 19, 20, 23)

hoípatȟe - fishing net; (pg 18, 20)

hoíyupsiče - fish hook; (pg 18)

hokhúwa - to fish, go fishing; (pg 23)

hónisko - to be noisy or loud

hóniskoskopi → **hónisko**; (pg 113)

hopášku - fish scales; (pg 105)

hoȟpí - a bird's nest; (pg 137)

hoští - I am in trouble! Too bad! Hard luck!; (pg 80, 130)

howákhuwa → **hokhúwa**; (pg 23)

hoyúȟ'i - tree ring; (pg 88)

hú - legs; (pg 11, 102, 103, 104, 105, 112, 116, 120)

hú matópa - I have four legs; (pg 102, 104)

huhú - bone, bones; (pg 52, 124, 125)

hukhúčiyela - to be short or low; (pg 89, 111)

húmastake → **hústakA**; (pg 99, 100)

húnistake → **hústakA**; (pg 99)

huŋhuŋhé - exclamation expressing a wide range of emotions, including pleasure and surprise; (pg 125)

húŋku - his/her mother; (pg 19, 20, 43, 80)

huŋská - leggings; (pg 52, 54, 59, 60)

huŋyákȟuŋ - socks; (pg 29)

hústakA - to be weary or tired in the leg; (pg 99, 100)

huští - I am in trouble! Too bad! Hard luck!; (pg 99)

ȟá - to bury smth/sb; (pg 10, 51, 104)

ȟáŋ - to have a sore or scab; (pg 25)

ȟanté - Rocky Mt. juniper, commonly called cedar; (pg 43, 89, 94, 95)

ȟaŋtkáŋoyuze - arm band; (pg 52)

ȟčA - really; (pg 38)

ȟčiŋ - really (pg 58, 62, 95, 112)

ȟé - mountain; (pg 51)

ȟláȟla - bells; (pg 51, 52)

ȟolȟótapi → **ȟótA**; (pg 112)

ȟóta - to be grey; (pg 51, 89)

ȟpáya - to lie, to be in a reclining position, to be lying;

ȟtálehaŋ - yesterday; (pg 129)

ȟupáhu - a bird's wing; (pg 102, 103, 105)

ȟwá - to be sleepy; (pg 43, 99, 127)

ȟ'aŋhí - to be slow; (pg 99)

ȟ'aŋhíya - slowly; (pg 99, 117)

ȟ'okȟá - traditional singer at a drum; (pg 62)

ȟ'úŋt'A - to be tired out by action, exhausted

í 1 - his/her/its mouth

í 2 - to arrive there, to have been there (pg 78)

iȟáȟa - to laugh at; (pg 51)

iȟát'A - to laugh hard

ibláble → **iyáyA**; (pg 80)

íblotakiŋ → **íyotakA**; (pg 59)

Glossary

ičábu - iyáwakaške

ičábu - drum stick; (pg 33, 48)

ičápsiŋte - a whip; (pg 12)

íčat'a - intensely, very much; (pg 42)

ičhíčiču → ikíču; (pg 134, 135, 137)

ičhíŋ - because, for you see, as you know; (pg 6, 80, 95, 110, 125)

ičínuŋpa - second; (pg 127, 128, 129, 131)

ičínuŋpani - not a second time; (pg 130)

ičíyamni - third; (pg 127, 128)

ičú - to take smth/sb; (pg 43, 44, 46, 49, 95, 100, 127, 133)

iglúš'iŋš'iŋ - to tickle oneself

iglúštaŋ - to finish or complete smth pertaining to oneself, to be through; (pg 43)

igmú - cat; (pg 117)

igmútȟaŋka - mountain lion; (pg 23, 24, 25, 95, 117)

igní - to search or hunt for smth; (pg 111, 113)

ihíŋhaŋni - the following morning; (pg 121)

ihúpa - a handle of something; (pg 94)

íipútȟake - to kiss sb; (pg 5)

ikȟáŋ - a rope; (pg 12, 91)

ikíču - to take smth for/from sb; (pg 132, 134, 135, 137)

ikíkču - to take one's own; (pg 46, 47, 49, 137)

ikȟóyakA - it is attached to smth; (pg 89)

Iktó - the trickster of Lakota myths; (pg 70)

Iktómi - the trickster of Lakota myths; (pg 94)

ilágwaye → ilágyA; (pg 23, 95)

ilágyA - to make use of smth/sb; (pg 23)

ilázata - behind smth/sb; (pg 24, 58)

iléyA - to make smth burn; (pg 41, 43)

imáhel - inside smth; (pg 89, 137)

imákiču → ikíču; (pg 124, 125, 130, 133, 134, 135)

ímapuza → ípuzA; (pg 80, 100)

imáyuŋǧe → iyúŋǧA; (pg 80)

iná - my mother; (pg 3, 19, 59)

ináȟni - to hurry; (pg 59, 99)

ináȟmA - to hide oneself; (pg 24)

ináwaȟme → ináȟmA; (pg 24)

iníkaǧA - to perform or participate in a purification ceremony (sweat lodge ceremony); (pg 43)

ínipuza → ípuzA; (pg 100)

ínipuziŋ → ípuzA; (pg 42)

iníthiyuktaŋ - dome-shaped booth made of bent willow saplings (used for the sweat lodge and for travois); (pg 94)

iŋchéye? - Right?, Isn't that so?; (pg 6, 137)

iŋš - as for him/her/it; (pg 6, 24, 80, 130)

iŋšé - only, just, merely; (pg 99)

iŋska - we...ll, so...; let me see (expression of hesitancy when not finding the right word at once); (pg 137)

iŋyaŋgyaŋg → íŋyaŋkA; (pg 130)

íŋyaŋkA - to run; (pg 28, 85, 111, 131)

íŋyaŋ - stone, rock; (pg 29, 41, 92, 93)

ípȟaȟte - a bridle; (pg 12)

ípuzA - to be thirsty; (pg 100, 122, 127)

iš'óš'oya - enthusiastically; (pg 108)

isákhib - next to smth/sb; (pg 81)

iškáhu - his/her/its ankle bone; (pg 52)

išláyatakiya - to the right side; (pg 81)

ištá - his/her/its eye, eyes; (pg 103, 104, 112, 116)

ištíŋmA - to sleep; (pg 113, 127)

istó - his/her/its arm; forearm; the foreleg of an animal; (pg 25)

itázipa - a bow; (pg 23, 94)

ité - his/her/its face; (pg 70, 112)

itéha - halter; (pg 12)

itéšniyaŋ! - really! seriously!; (pg 110)

ithíčaǧapi - to set smth up (as a tent); (pg 39)

itípakhiŋte - a towel; (pg 49)

itȟókab - in front of smth/sb, before smth/sb; (pg 60)

itȟúŋkala - mouse; (pg 29, 36, 101, 116, 117, 125)

itȟúŋkasaŋ - weasel; (pg 117)

iwékču → ikíkču; (pg 47, 48, 49, 59, 137)

iwíčhaču → ičú; (pg 121)

iwíčhawaču → ičú; (pg 121)

iyáȟpayA - to jump on smth/sb; (pg 25)

iyákaškA - to tie smth to smth; (pg 12)

iyámaȟpaye → iyáȟpayA; (pg 25)

iyániȟpaya → iyáȟpayA; (pg 25)

iyáwakaške → iyákaškA; (pg 13)

iyáyA - to have left, to leave, to start; (pg 43, 75, 78, 81, 83, 94, 127)

iyáye → **iyáyA**

iyáyiŋ → **iyáyA**

iyéčhel - like smth/sb; (pg 117)

iyéčhiŋkyaŋke - car; (pg 6, 59, 60, 135)

iyékču → **ikíču**; (pg 47, 48)

iyékiyA - to find one's own; (pg 58)

iyéwakiye → **iyékiyA**; (pg 58)

iyéwaye → **iyéyA**; (pg 80)

iyéwičhawaye → **iyéyA**; (pg 121)

iyéwičhaye → **iyéyA**; (pg 121)

iyéyA - to find smth/sb; (pg 80); (pg 121)

iyóȟa - gills (of fish); (pg 105)

iyóhila - each, every; (pg 121)

iyóhomni - around smth/sb; (pg 41)

iyókphi - to be pleased or happy; (pg 70)

iyókišičA - to be sad; (pg 122)

iyópteya - straight on, straight through; (pg 81, 82)

íyotakA - to sit down; (pg 59, 86)

iyótaŋš - especially; (pg 117)

iyúha - all; (pg 80, 114, 115)

iyúŋǧA - to ask sb about smth; (pg 94)

iyúŋg → **iyúŋkA, iyúŋgkhiyA**; (pg 122)

iyúŋgkhiyA → to put sb to bed; (pg 122)

iyúŋg-wičhúŋkhiya → **iyúŋgkhiyA**; (pg 122)

iyúŋkA - to lie down, go to bed, go to sleep; (pg 128)

iyúškiŋyaŋ - happily; (pg 127)

iyútȟA - to try smth, taste smth; (pg 127)

izítA - it rises (ex: smoke); (pg 43)

ká - there (away from the speaker and listener); (pg 70, 110)

kač'úŋ - because of too much of; (pg 108)

káǧA - to make smth; (pg 51, 52, 94, 95, 129, 136)

kaká - my grandpa (northern); (pg 38)

kaksáksa - to chop smth with an ax; (pg 41, 42)

kaksÁ - to cut smth with an ax

kál - there (away from the speaker and listener); (pg 95)

kaná - those over there (away from speaker and listener); (pg 95)

kap'óšp'ožela → **kap'óžela; (pg 108)**

kap'óžela - to be light of weight; (pg 92, 97)

kastó - to groom smth/sb, to smooth smth down (as hair); (pg 12, 13)

kaú - to be bringing smth/sb; (pg 136)

kaúŋspe - to train smth/sb; (pg 12)

kazó - to draw a line; (pg 80)

kayéžu - to pay for smth; (pg 80)

ke → **táku ke éyaš**; (pg 117)

kéčhiŋ - to think that; (pg 111)

képȟe → **kéyA**; (pg 96)

kéyA - to say that; (pg 70, 96)

khes'ámna - musk turtle, stink turtle; (pg 108)

khéya - turtle; (pg 10, 70, 109)

khí 1 - to take smth away from sb; (pg 12, 70)

khí 2 - to arrive back there

khilí - to be awesome, cool; to be extreme/exceeding; (pg 06, 43)

khíza - to fight sb; (pg 70)

khukhúše - pig; (pg 70)

khuté - to shoot at sb/smth; (pg 23, 25)

khuwá - to chase smth/sb, to treat sb in some way; (pg 16, 22, 23, 25, 27, 38, 62, 70)

kȟÁ - to mean smth/sb, to imply smth; (pg 22)

kȟalkȟáte → **kȟátA**; (pg 91, 93, 96)

kȟalyÁ - to heat smth; (pg 96)

kȟaŋǧí - crow; (pg 95)

kȟáŋmat'e → **kȟáŋt'A**; (pg 60)

kȟáŋta - plum; (pg 30, 90, 94, 95, 96, 133)

kȟáŋt'A - to be frustrated; (pg 60)

kȟáŋtahu čháŋ - plum tree; (pg 90, 95)

kȟátA - it is hot/warm; (pg 91, 96, 127, 128)

kȟó - too, also, as well; (pg 117)

kȟolá - my friend; (pg 96)

kȟoškálaka - young man; (pg 16, 96)

kȟúŋšitku - his/her grandmother; (pg 79, 96)

ki- - affix for the dative (for, from, to); (pg 133, 134)

kič'úŋ - to put on and wear one's own; (pg 59, 108)

kíčaǧA - to make smth for sb; U3 (pg.43, 136)

Glossary

kičhí - with him/her; (pg 24, 25, 43, 45, 74, 75, 76, 77, 83, 85, 87)

kigléǧA - to overtake sb, sth, to catch up with; (pg 16, 22, 23)

kiktá - to get up, to wake; (pg 113, 120, 130, 131)

kiktá-hiyáyA - to get up quickly or suddenly; (pg 130, 131)

kilówaŋ - to sing to/for sb; (pg 5)

kimímela - butterfly; (pg 70, 118)

kiŋ - the

kiŋyÁŋ - to fly; (pg 120)

kiŋyékhiyapi - an airplane; (pg 6, 129)

kipázo - to show smth to sb; (pg 136)

kítaŋla - a little, in a slight degree; (pg 38, 43, 100, 128)

kiúŋ - to use smth that belongs to sb; (pg 130)

kiyáȟepA - to drink smth that belongs to sb; (pg 136, 137)

kiyátkAŋ - to drink smth that belongs to sb; (pg 136)

kiyúǧaŋ - to open smth for/on sb; (pg 136)

kiyúšičA - to damage smth that pertains to sb; (pg 137)

kiyútA - to eat smth that belongs to sb; (pg 136)

kízA - to creak; (pg 70)

kózA - to wave smth; (pg 70)

kpahí - to pick one's own; (pg 50, 54)

kpaŋyÁŋ - to tan smth (as a hide), dress a hide; (pg 28)

kpazó - to show one's own; (pg 49, 54, 55)

kštó - indicates an assertion

ktA - marks a future or possible event

kú - to be coming back; (pg 31, 43, 70)

kúŋ - to covet smth/sb; (pg 70)

k'á - to dig smth; (pg 108)

k'éyaš - but; (pg 108, 133)

k'íŋ - to carry smth/sb; (pg 108)

k'ó - there is noise and excitement; (pg 108)

k'ú - to give smth to sb; (pg 4, 32,19, 20, 80, 101, 108)

k'uŋ - the aforesaid; (pg 95)

lá 1 → yÁ; (pg 99)

lá 2 - to ask for smth

lalá - my grandpa (southern variant); (pg 38)

latkíŋ → yatkÁŋ; (pg 43)

lawápi → yawá; (pg 62)

lé 1 - this (near the speaker)

lé 2 → yÁ

lečháŋmi → lečhíŋ; (pg 80)

léchel - this way, in this manner; (pg 13)

léchiya - here; (pg 43)

lečhíŋ - to think this (precedes a quote); (pg 79)

lekší - my uncle

lená - these (near the speaker); (pg 93)

líglila - each time very → líla; (pg 62)

líla - very, a lot

ló - assertion, spoken by a man

ločhíŋ - to be hungry; (pg 27, 43, 85, 99, 118, 121, 127)

lol'íȟ'aŋ - to cook; (pg 39)

lowáčhiŋ → ločhíŋ; (pg 80, 85, 133, 137)

lowáŋ - to sing; (pg 32, 62)

loyáčhiŋ → ločhíŋ; (pg 42, 99)

luȟíče-ȟča → yuȟíčA; (pg 38)

lulyÁ - to dye smth; (pg 119)

lúzahAŋ - to be fleet footed; (pg 120)

má! - Look! Why! Here! Say! Gee! (pg 110)

mačháŋzeke → čhaŋzékA; (pg 60, 95)

mačhépe → čhépA; (pg 99)

mačhúwita → čhuwíta; (pg 99,100)

mačíkčik'ala → čík'ala; (pg 103)

maǧáŋ → ǧáŋ; (pg 100)

maǧážu - it is raining; (pg 85)

maǧí → ǧí; (pg 104)

magmígmigma → gmigmá; (pg 103)

maháŋskaska → háŋskA (pg 103)

maháŋske → háŋskA; (pg 104)

maháŋskiŋ → háŋskA; (pg 103)

mahél - inside; (pg 60, 101)

mahétaŋhaŋ - from within; → čhaŋhá mahétaŋhaŋ; (pg 117)

mahí → él mahí – he came to me; → hí; (pg 59)

mak'ú → k'ú; (pg 5, 22, 33)

makȟátomniča - wild bean; (pg 124)

makáu → kaú; (pg 40)

makȟé → kȟÁ; (pg 22)

makȟínapte - a shovel; (pg 41)

makȟíze → khízA; (pg)

makhúte → khuté; (pg)

makhúwa → **khuwá**; (pg 25)

makípazo → **kipázo**; (pg)

makíuŋ → **kiúŋ**; (pg 130)

makíyaȟepe → **kiyáȟepA**; (pg 130)

makíyatke → **kiyátkAŋ**; (pg 136)

makíyuǧaŋ → **kiyúǧaŋ**; (pg 137)

makíyušiče → **kiyúšičA**; (pg 124)

makíyute → **kiyútA**; (pg 130)

makígleǧe → **kigléǧA**; (pg 22)

máni - to walk; (pg 40, 108, 121)

maníče → **níčA**; (pg 80,137)

mapȟépȟe → **pȟé**; (pg 103)

mapȟéstola → **pȟéstola**; (pg 104)

maptéčela → **ptéčela**; (pg 104)

mašákowiŋ → **šakówiŋ**; (pg 58)

masáŋ → **sáŋ**; (pg 103)

masápsapiŋ → **sápA**; (pg 103)

masčháŋyapȟa → bridle bits; (pg 12)

maswígmuŋke - iron trap or snare; (pg 23)

mas'ákipȟA - to give someone a phone call; (pg 21, 136)

mas'ámakipȟe → **mas'ákipȟA**; (pg 6, 22)

mas'áničipȟa → **mas'ákipȟA**; (pg 22)

mas'ápȟA - to make a phone call; (pg 136)

mas'ínaȟtake - spurs; (pg 12)

mašápe → **šápA**; (pg 100)

maškópe → **škópA**; (pg 103)

matȟáŋka → **tȟáŋka**; (pg 104)

matȟáŋkiŋkiŋyaŋ → **tȟáŋka**; (pg 103)

matȟápiȟ'a - toad; (pg 103, 116)

matȟó - bear; (pg 95, 119, 125, 130)

matópa → **tópa**; (pg 102, 104)

maúŋni → **máni**; (pg 86, 99)

maȟwá → **ȟwá**; (pg 99)

mawáni → **máni**; (pg 24)

mawániče → **wanícA**; (pg 102, 103, 104)

mayák'u → **k'ú**; (pg 32, 33, 34)

mayákiyuǧaŋ → **kiyúǧaŋ**; (pg 137)

mayáluȟiča → **yuȟíčA**; (pg 38)

mayáȟtake → **yaȟtákA**; (pg 25)

mayúȟ'i → **yuȟ'í**; (pg 103,104)

mayúȟiče → **yuȟíčA**; (pg 38)

mayúkȟe → **yukȟÁŋ**; (pg 102, 106)

mayúȟlate → **yuȟlátA**; (pg 25)

mayúwi → **yuwí**; (pg 25)

mayúze → **napé yúzA**, **pȟóskil yúzA**; (pg 5, 7, 8)

mázaská thípi - bank; (pg 74, 81)

mázaškaŋškaŋ - clock, o'clock; (pg 49)

mázasu - bullet; (pg 23)

mázawakȟáŋ - gun; (pg 23)

mazí → **zí**; (pg 103)

mignáka - to wear smth in the belt (as a knife-case); → **pȟeží mignáka**; (pg 58, 60)

míla - knife; (pg 18, 19, 91)

miméla - to be round; (pg 116)

mimémelapi → **miméla**; (pg 112, 116)

míožuha - knife case; (pg 53)

mitȟáŋkala - my little sister (woman speaking); (pg 124)

mitȟáwa - my, mine

míyoglas'iŋ - mirror; (pg 108)

mní - water; (pg 18, 33, 41, 100, 137)

mnik'ú - to give water to sb/smth; (pg 121)

mnikápȟopapi - soda, pop; (pg 80, 100, 101)

Mnikȟáta - Hot Springs, SD; (pg 68)

mníŋ → **yÁ**; (pg 62, 72, 73, 80, 84, 95, 110)

mniš'éš'e - to sprinkle, to rain gently; (pg 108)

mniskúya - salt; (pg 117)

mniwák'u → **mnik'ú**; (pg 13)

mniwíčhak'u → **mnik'ú**; (pg 121)

mniwíčhuŋk'u → **mnik'ú**; (pg 122)

na - and

naȟ'úŋ - to hear smth/sb; (pg 16, 22)

naháŋ - and; (pg 112)

naíč'ižiŋ - to defend oneself; (pg 108)

naíŋš - or; (pg 24, 94, 112, 117)

nakéš - finally; (pg 42)

nakpá - external ears; (pg 103, 105, 112, 114, 115, 116)

naȟmá - to hide smth/sb; (pg 113)

naȟtákA - to kick smth/sb; (pg 38)

Glossary

namáȟtake → **naȟtákA**; (pg 7)

naníȟ'uŋ → **naȟ'úŋ**; (pg 22, 24)

naŋkíŋ → **yaŋkÁ**; (pg 42)

napȟÁ - to flee, run away; (pg 23, 130)

napȟé → **napȟÁ**; (pg 27)

napé - his/her hand; (pg 54, 105)

napé yúzA - to shake sb's hand; (pg 7)

napȟéyA - to scare sb/smth away; (pg 96)

napókaške - wristlet; (pg 52)

napsú - his/her finger; (pg 112)

natá - his/her head; (pg 101, 103, 112, 115, 116)

nawápȟe → **napȟÁ**; (pg 25)

nážiŋ - to stand; (pg 14, 32)

nazúŋspe - ax; (pg 41)

ni- - you; (pg 19, 22)

ní 1 - I wish, see: **tókhe … ní**; (pg 43)

ní 2 - to live

niȟ'áŋhi → **ȟ'aŋhí**; (pg 99)

nič'ú → **k'ú**; (pg 19, 22, 33, 45)

ničháŋzeke → **čhaŋzékA**; (pg 99)

ničhépe → **čhépA**; (pg 99)

ničhúwa → **khuwá**; (pg 22, 25)

ničhúwita → **čhuwíta**; (pg 99, 100)

ničígleǧe → **kigléǧA**; (pg 22)

ničípazo → **kipázo**; (pg 135)

ničíyaȟepe → **kiyáȟepA**; (pg 137)

ničíyuǧaŋ → **kiyúǧaŋ**; (pg 137)

niǧáŋ → **ǧáŋ**; (pg 100)

nihíŋčiyA - to be frightened or scared; (pg 43)

nikȟúŋši → **uŋčí**; (pg 19, 79)

níŋ → **yÁ**; (pg 42, 72, 73)

níš - you indeed; (pg 48, 59, 60 99)

níš tók - how about you; (pg 48, 60, 62, 68)

nišápe → **šápA**; (pg 100)

níš-eyá - you too; (pg 60, 62)

ništíŋmiŋ → **ištíŋmA**; (pg 42)

nitáku → **táku**; (pg 102, 103, 104)

nitȟáwa - your, yours; (pg 42, 137)

nitȟó - familiar command spoken by a woman, see **yetȟó**; (pg 135)

nitóna → **tóna**; (pg 102, 103, 104)

niȟwá → **ȟwá**; (pg 42, 99)

niyáȟtaka → **yaȟtákA**; (pg 25)

niyáte → **até**; (pg 19, 20)

niyé - you; (pg 42, 77)

niyúkȟaŋ → **yukȟÁŋ**; (pg 102, 103)

niyúwi → **yuwí**; (pg 25)

núŋm - two; (pg 116, 133)

núŋpa - two; (pg 120)

nuŋwÁŋ - to swim; (pg 62, 63, 65, 67, 85, 87)

nuphíŋ - both; (pg 68)

ó - to shoot and hit smth/sb; (pg 23, 25)

oȟ'áŋkȟo - to be fast; (pg 78)

oȟ'áŋkȟoya - quickly; (pg 117)

oákaŋke - chair; (pg 47, 58, 100)

obláke → **oyákA**; (pg 38)

očhéthi - fireplace, firepit; (pg 41, 42)

óčhičiyiŋ → **ókiyA**; (pg 95)

očhíyake → **oyákA**; (pg 38)

očhíyuspiŋ → **oyúspA**; (pg 36)

očhósya - warmly, comfortably, cozily, snugly; (pg 127)

oglákA - to tell one's own; (pg 62)

ógle - shirt; (pg 52, 128)

ógle zigzíča - sweater; (pg 137)

oglúspA - to hold onto one's own, to catch one's own; (pg 50, 54)

ogná - in, within; (pg 59)

ognákA - to put smth in smth; (pg 43)

oháŋ - okay, OK; (pg 76, 77, 80, 84, 85, 95, 10, 122, 125, 134)

óhiŋniyaŋ - always; (pg 62, 63, 69, 99)

ohúŋkakaŋ - a mythological story of the very remote past; (pg 98)

óič'iye - he helped himself; → **ókiyA**; (pg 108)

oíčhimani thípi - hotel; (pg 74, 82)

oínažiŋ → **wígli oínažiŋ**, **pȟéta oínažiŋ**; (pg 74, 80)

oíse-yámni - a triangle; (pg 90)

oíyokpas áye - it is getting dark; (pg 98)

okȟátA - to be hot; (pg 100)

okȟáŋ - to have time; (pg 80)

okȟólawaya → **okȟólayA**; (pg 60)

okȟólayA - to have sb for a friend; (pg 60)

okíhi - can, be able to; (pg 110)

okíle - to look for one's own; (pg 50)

ókiyA - to help sb; (pg 16, 95)

ókšaŋ - around smth/sb; (pg 58, 80)

ok'ú - to lend smth to sb; (pg 60)

oláke → **oyákA**; (pg 36, 38)

olé - to look for smth/sb; (pg 94, 110)

olówaŋ omnáye - IPod; (pg 49)

omák'u → **ok'ú**; (pg 59)

omákȟaŋ → **okȟáŋ**; (pg 80)

omákȟate → **okȟátA**; (pg 100)

ómakiye → **ókiyA**; (pg 22, 25)

omále → **olé**; (pg)

ómamna → **ómna**; (pg 25)

ománi - to travel, to walk about; (pg 127)

omáyake → **oyákA**; (pg 38)

omáyalaka → **oyákA**; (pg 38)

omáyaluspiŋ → **oyúspA**; (pg 36)

omáyuspe → **oyúspA**; (pg 22, 57)

ómna - to smell smth/sb; (pg 23)

omnáye → **wóuŋspe omnáye, olówaŋ omnáye**

óničiya → **ókiyA**; (pg 25)

oníkȟate → **okȟátA**; (pg 100)

ónimna → **ómna**; (pg 25)

onúŋwe thípi - indoors swimming pool; (pg 62)

oómna - smell, aroma; (pg 113)

oówa - color; (pg 134)

ópȟa - to take part in smth (used with **él**: **él ópȟA**) (pg 14, 58)

opȟékičatȟuŋ - to buy smth for sb; (pg 136)

opȟétȟuŋ - to buy smth; (pg 80, 136)

opȟéwatȟuŋ → **opȟétȟuŋ**; (pg 80)

ópta - across smth; (pg 82)

óptakiya - to go across smth; (pg 82)

oštéka → **aǧúyapi oštéka**; (pg 80)

óta - many; (pg 13, 116)

othí → **pteyúha othí, owáyazaŋ othí, wičhítenaškaŋškaŋ othí, wówapi othí**

otȟáb - following or tracking smth/sb; (pg 121)

otȟámapȟa → **otȟápȟA**; (pg 25)

otȟápȟA - to track sb/smth, follow; (pg 23)

otȟókaheya - at first, for the first time; (pg 43)

otȟúŋwahe - town; (pg 43)

otȟúŋwahetakiya - towards the town; (pg 131)

otkéyA - to hang smth up; (pg 40)

otútuya - in vain; (pg 70)

owáčhekiye - church; (pg 74, 79)

owágluspe → **oglúspA**; (pg 50)

owák'u → **ok'ú**; (pg 60)

owákile → **okíle**; (pg 47, 49)

ówakiye → **ókiyA**; (pg 60)

owákšiyužaža - sink; (pg 60)

owále → **olé**; (pg 86, 95)

Owáŋgyužažapi - Saturday; (pg 13)

owáŋyaŋkA - to look like (a certain way); (pg 112)

ówapȟa → **ópȟa**; (pg 14, 58)

owáyawa - school; (pg 62, 73)

owáyazaŋ othí - hospital; (pg 73, 74, 76, 77, 79)

óweháŋhaŋ - jokingly, in a teasing manner; (pg 99)

owíčhayake → **oyákA** (to tell on them); (pg 38)

owíŋla - earrings; (pg 53)

owíŋža - bedding; quilt, blanket; (pg 18, 20, 33, 42, 46)

owíyopȟeye - a store or stall to sell smth; (pg 80)

owótȟaŋla - to be straight; (pg 81, 92)

owóte thípi - restaurant; (pg 73)

oyáglakiŋ → **oglákA**; (pg 42)

oyákA - to tell on sb/smth, to report smth/sb, relate smth; (pg 36, 38)

oyé - tracks of a specified animal; (pg 23, 25, 110)

oyúspA - to catch sb/smth; to grab, to hold onto; (pg 23, 36 50, 54, 61)

oyúžužu thípi - post office; (pg 74)

ožáŋžaŋglepi - window; (pg 131)

pablú - to burrow; (pg 70)

paȟá - hill; (pg 32, 70)

paháta - at/in the hills; (pg 32)

pahí - to pick smth/sb; (pg 41, 95)

Glossary

paílepi - flashlight; (pg 18)

paŋȟyá - very, whole bunch, a lot; (pg 25, 133)

pathíma - pushing smth inside; (pg 101)

pazó - to show smth, point smth out; (pg 49)

pe - female command; (pg 76)

pemní - it is twisted; (pg 70)

philámayaye - thank you (pg 135)

phizí - gall; (pg 70)

pȟahíŋ - porcupine; porcupine quilt; (pg 95, 110, 111, 112, 113, 117, 118, 119)

pȟaŋkéska - abalone; (pg 43)

pȟaŋšpȟáŋžela → pȟáŋžela; (pg 96)

pȟáŋžela - to be soft; (pg 92)

pȟapȟá 1 - to bark at sb/smth; (pg 14, 16, 17)

pȟapȟá 2 - it is bitter; (pg 96)

pȟasú - his/her nose, its beak; (pg 96, 103, 105)

pȟátA - to butcher smth; (pg 27)

pȟeháŋ - crane (bird); (pg 37)

pȟatkáša - western painted turtle; (pg 105)

pȟé - to be sharp; (pg 91), (pg 112)

pȟepȟé → pȟé; (pg 91), (pg 112)

pȟešá - headroach; (pg 52)

pȟešníža - ember; (pg 91)

pȟéstola - to be sharp pointed; (pg 91)

pȟestóstolapi → pȟéstola; (pg 120)

pȟéta - fire; (pg 41, 42)

pȟéta oínažiŋ - fire station; (pg 74)

pȟeží - grass; (pg 12, 60, 119)

pȟeží mignáka - grass dance; (pg. 60)

pȟežíȟota - sage; (pg 40)

pȟežúta - medicine, pill; (pg 100)

pȟóskil yúze - to hug sb; (pg 5, 6), (pg 121, 122)

pȟóštaŋ - to put smth on one's head; (pg 101)

-pi - affix marking animate plural; (pg 8)

pispíza - prairie dog; (pg 70)

píza - to squeak (ex: a mouse); (pg 70)

po/pe - marks a command given to more than one people; (pg 101)

póǧaŋ - to blow on smth (with the mouth); (pg 41, 42)

pséȟtiŋ - the ash tree; (pg 89)

ptaŋyétu - fall; (pg 113)

pté - buffalo; (pg 70)

ptéčela - to be short; (pg 89, 129)

ptehíŋšma - buffalo robe with fur left on it; (pg 127)

ptepȟá - buffalo skull; (pg 33, 101)

pteptéčela → ptéčela; (pg 95)

pteyúha othí - a farm; (pg 17, 83)

pusyÁ - to dry smth; (pg 40, 119)

púzA - to be dry; (pg 70)

p'é - elm; (pg 108)

p'éčhaŋ - elm tree; (pg 108)

p'ó - fog; (pg 108)

p'oyéla - foggy; (pg 108)

sagyé - a cane, walking stick; (pg 122)

sáŋ - to be dull white, off-white, whitish or grayish white; (pg 29, 103)

sápA - to be black; (pg 13, 112, 122)

sapsápapi → sápA; (pg 112)

séčA - maybe, possibly, it might be so; (pg 58)

sí - his/her/its foot; (pg 103)

sičhóla - to be barefoot; (pg 59)

siínataŋ - stirrups; (pg 12)

siŋkpȟé - muskrat; (pg 117)

siŋté - its tail; (pg 102, 105)

siŋtéȟla - rattlesnake; (pg 29)

siŋtúpi - its tail feathers; (pg 103, 105)

siókaza - his/her/its toes; (pg 105,112)

sítȟapa škátapi - football; (pg 65)

ská - to be white; (pg 70)

skaská → ská; (pg 89)

skúyA - to be sweet; (pg 128)

slol'úŋyaŋpi → slolyÁ; (pg 133)

slol'úŋye → slolyÁ; (pg 86)

slolwáye → slolyÁ; (pg 133)

slolyÁ - to know smth/sb; (pg 86, 133)

snásna - to jingle, ring; (pg 122)

sní - it (a thing) is cold; (pg 122)

so - marks conversational informal question, often used

when the questioner does not expect an answer; (pg 94)

sóso - to cut smth into thin and long strips; (pg 122)

spáyA - to be wet; (pg 70)

stákA - one's body part is tired or weary; (pg 70)

sú - seed; (pg 88, 92, 124)

sutá - to be hard; (pg 92)

s'a - often; (pg 62, 63, 99)

s'amná - to stink; (pg 108)

s'e - as though, as if, like; (pg 108)

s'elé - it seems; (pg 108)

s'eléčheča - it seems; (pg 112)

s'íŋs'iŋyaŋ - gulping; (pg 108)

šá - to be red; (pg 89, 134)

šabšápapi → **šápA**; (pg 121)

šaké - his/her finger nails, claws, hooves; (pg 105, 102)

šakówiŋ - seven

šákpe - six; (pg 122)

šápA - to be dirty; (pg 100, 121, 122)

šašté - his/her little finger; (pg 122)

šič'éku - her brother-in-law; (pg 108)

šičámna - to smell bad; (pg 127)

šiná - blanket, shawl; (pg 48, 122, 127)

šišóka - robin; (pg 122)

šiyótȟaŋka - flute; (pg 39)

škáŋ - to act or move about; (pg 42)

škátA - to play; (pg 85, 85)

škhé - it is said; (pg 130)

škȟá - and yet; (pg 127)

škópA - to be bent in a gentle curve, hooked; (pg 92, 103, 112, 116)

škoškópapi → **škópA**; (pg 112)

šlušlútA - to be slippery; polished, smooth, shining; (pg 122)

šna - usually; (pg 62, 63, 68, 94, 111, 113, 117)

šni - not

šókA - to be thin; (pg 127)

šokšóke → **šókA**; (pg 95)

šóta - smoke; to smoke (as fire), to send out smoke; (pg 41)

šuŋǧíla - red fox; (pg 37)

šuŋgléška - spotted horse, pinto; (pg 13)

šuŋgmánitu - coyote; (pg 117)

šuŋgsápA - black horse; (pg 13)

šuŋgská - white horse; (pg 13)

šuŋkšáke - horse hoof; (pg 105)

šuŋk'ákaŋyaŋkA - to ride horseback; (pg 12, 13, 65, 68)

šuŋk'óye - horse tracks; (pg 121)

šúŋka - dog; (pg 14, 16, 114, 124)

šúŋkawakȟáŋ - horse; (pg 8, 12, 14, 15, 114, 115)

šuŋksímaza - horseshoe; (pg 11)

šuŋksíŋte - horse tail; (pg 11)

šuŋksíšake - horse hoof; (pg 11)

šuŋȟpála - puppy; (pg 121)

šutȟÁ - to miss aim in shooting at smth/sb; (pg 23, 27)

š'á - din, a confused sound; (pg 108)

š'agš'ákapi → **š'ákA**; (pg 112)

š'ákA - it is strong/powerful (of body parts); (pg 112, 116)

š'é - drops are dripping; (pg 108)

š'éš'e → **š'é**; (pg 108)

-ta - at, to; (pg 73)

táku - what; something; (pg 70)

táku ke éyaš - anything; (pg 117)

tákuni - nothing; (pg 33, 42, 43)

takúŋl - something (potential); (pg 60, 127, 128)

tákuwe - why; (pg 32, 38, 95, 120)

taŋtáŋyaŋ → **taŋyáŋ**; (pg 114)

taŋyáŋ - well; to be well; it is good that; (pg 6, 113, 114)

taŋyáŋkel - fairly well; (pg 113)

theȟíla - to love smth/sb; (pg 22, 70)

themáȟila → **theȟíla**; (pg 7, 22)

thezí - his/her/its stomach or belly; (pg 122)

thí - to live (as in a place, area or house); (pg 72, 79)

thibló - my older brother (female speaking); (pg 43)

thiblóku - her older brother; (pg 124)

thiíkčeya - tipi; (pg 127)

thimá - inside, in a house or tent; (pg 80, 127)

thípi 1 - they live, → **thí**;

thípi 2 - house; (pg 70)

thiyáta - at home; (pg 28, 130)

thiyátakiya - towards home; (pg 131)

Glossary

thiyóbleǧa - a tent; (pg 18, 19)

thiyóle - visiting in order to eat; (pg 70)

thiyópa - a door; (pg 70)

thukíha - shell (without the animal); (pg 105)

tȟaló - meat; (pg 28)

tȟaŋčháŋ - his/her/its body; (pg 113)

tȟaŋháŋši - my male cousin (male speaking); (pg 59)

tȟáŋka - to be large, big, great; (pg 104, 113, 124)

tȟaŋkál - outside; (pg 76)

tȟaŋkší - my younger sister (male speaking); (pg 96)

tȟaŋníla - it is old (of inanimate things); (pg 96)

tȟabškátA - to play basketball; (pg 35, 62, 68)

tȟahá čhuwígnaka - buckskin dress; (pg 53)

tȟahú - his/her/its neck; (pg 52)

tȟakóža - my grandchild; (pg 122)

tȟáȟča - deer; (pg 27)

tȟáȟča oyé - deer tracks; (pg 23)

tȟápa - ball; (pg 91)

tȟaspáŋ - apple; (pg 56)

tȟašúpa - intestines; (pg 96)

tȟáwa - his/her/its; (pg 54, 96, 133)

tȟebkhíyA - to eat up smth that belongs to sb; (pg 136)

tȟebkíyA - to eat one's own up; (pg 137)

tȟebmákhiye → tȟebkhíyA; (pg 125, 137)

tȟebwákhiye → tȟebkhíyA; (pg 137)

tȟebwáye → tȟebyÁ; (pg 80)

tȟebyÁ - to eat smth up; (pg 110, 111, 136)

tȟéča - to be new, be young; (pg 44)

tȟéhaŋ - for a long time; (pg 96)

tȟektȟéhaŋl → tȟéhaŋ; (pg 14)

tȟoká - enemy; (pg 14, 15, 81)

tȟokáheya - first; (pg 43, 119, 127, 129)

tȟothó → tȟó; (pg 89)

tȟuŋkášitku - his/her grandfather; (pg 33)

tȟuŋwíŋ - my aunt; (pg 65)

tkȟá - but; used to; (pg 60)

tké - to be heavy; (pg 92)

tketké → tké; (pg 93)

tȟó - to be blue; (pg 63)

tȟokéya - first, at first; (pg 41, 80)

tób → tópa; (pg 32)

tóhaŋ - when (in the past); (pg 22, 112)

tóhaŋȟčiŋ - when, ever; (pg 111)

tóhaŋni - never; (pg 62, 63)

toháŋtuka waŋ - once, once upon a time; (pg 127)

tók - how about it?; (pg 62)

tókča - what is it like?; (pg 103, 104)

tókhe ... ní - I wish; (pg 43)

tókheni ... šni - to be unable to; (pg 59)

tókheškhe - how; (pg 41)

tókhetkiya - in what direction, in some direction; (pg 131)

tókhiya - where, to where; (pg 32)

tókȟa - in táku tókȟa he? – What is going on? What is wrong? What is up?; (pg 95)

tókȟa šni - never mind, it doesn't matter; (pg 95)

tókȟa (verb) šni - to be unable to; (pg 95)

tókȟaȟ'aŋ - to disappear; (pg 59)

tókȟamuŋ → tókȟuŋ; (pg 42)

tókȟanuŋ → tókȟuŋ; (pg 60, 110)

tókȟuŋ - to do what; (pg 62, 101, 126)

tóna - how many; several; (pg 32)

toníkča → tókča; (pg 103, 116)

tópa - four, to be four; (pg 102), (pg 112)

tukté waŋží - which one; (pg 32)

tuktená - which ones from a group; (pg 117)

tuktétu - where is it, it is somewhere; (pg 62)

tuwá - who; (pg 3, 4, 22)

tuwéni - no one; (pg 38, 133)

tuwéni šni - there is no one; (pg 127)

t'Á - to be dead, to die; (pg 108)

t'at'áič'iyA - to relax; (pg 108)

t'ečá - to be lukewarm (as water); tepid; (pg 108)

t'osyéla - giving a dull sound; (pg 108)

t'uŋgyÁ - to suspect smth/sb; (pg 108)

ú - to be coming; (pg 135)

uŋ 1 - using, with, (pg 15, 16, 43, 54, 85, 94, 95, 101, 119)

úŋ 2 - to use or wear smth; (pg 29, 136, 137, 133)

úŋ 3 - to be, to live; (pg 58, 59, 60, 86, 101)

uŋ 4 → čha hé uŋ

uŋčí - my grandmother; (pg 44)

uŋgná - maybe; (pg 41)

uŋgnáhaŋla - suddenly; (pg 27)

uŋk'íŋyaŋke → íŋyaŋkA; (pg 86)

uŋk'íŋyaŋkiŋ → íŋyaŋkA; (pg 110)

uŋk'úŋpi → úŋ; (pg 108)

uŋkáǧiŋ → káǧA; (pg 95)

uŋkčékhiħa - magpie; (pg 105)

uŋkčéla - cactus; (pg 52)

uŋkíču → iču; (pg 95)

uŋkínaȟni → ináȟni; (pg 98)

uŋkípi → í; (pg 59)

uŋkóle → olé; (pg 86, 110)

uŋmáspe → uŋspé; (pg 65)

uŋníspe → uŋspé; (pg 61, 65, 66)

uŋnúŋwaŋpi → nuŋwÁŋ; (pg 68, 87)

uŋnúŋwiŋ → nuŋwÁŋ; (pg 87)

uŋpáhi → pahí; (pg 95)

úŋpi → úŋ; (pg 94, 113)

uŋškátiŋ → škátA; (pg 85)

uŋspé - to know how to do smth; (pg 65)

uŋspéčhičhiyiŋ → uŋspékhiyA; (pg 39)

uŋspékhiyA - to teach smth to sb; (pg 63)

uŋspémakhiye → uŋspékhiyA; (pg 43)

uŋspémayakhiyiŋ → uŋspékhiyA; (pg 39)

uŋspéničhiyiŋ → uŋspékhiyA; (pg 39)

uŋyáŋ - you and I go; → yÁ; (pg 74, 80)

uŋyáŋkiŋ → yaŋkÁ; (pg 85)

uŋyáŋpi → yÁ; (pg 24, 84)

uŋyíŋ → yÁ; (pg 74)

uŋyútiŋ → yútA; (pg 118, 119)

uŋzóǧe - pants; (pg 6, 128)

phuté - its snout, his/her upper lip; (pg 105)

waȟ'áŋič'ila - be haughty, to think highly of oneself; (pg 108)

waákhita - to be on the lookout, look around, scan about; (pg 23, 27)

waápȟA - to hit people; (pg 38)

waákhipȟa - to experience certain events; (pg 41)

waáwakhipȟa → waákhipȟa; (pg 41)

wábloša - red-winged blackbird; (pg 94)

wačhékiyA - to pray; (pg 40)

wačhéyakiyiŋ → wačhékiyA; (pg 41)

wačhéye → čhéyA; (pg 60)

wačhí - to dance; (pg 60, 64)

wáčhiŋhiŋ - plume, down or soft feather; (pg 53)

wačhíŋkȟo - to pout; (pg 96)

wačhípi - a dance; they dance; → wačhí; (pg 39)

wáǧačhaŋ - cottonwood; (pg 90, 93)

wagláȟepe → glaȟépA; (pg 137)

waglékšuŋ - turkey; (pg 24, 117)

waglí → glí; (pg 13)

waglúǧaŋ → gluǧáŋ; (pg 137)

waglúha → gluhá; (pg 49)

waglútiŋ → glútA; (pg 56)

waglúžaža → glužáža; (pg 59)

wagmíza - corn; (pg 80)

wagmúšpaŋšni - watermelon; (pg 80)

wagnúni → gnúni; (pg 58)

wahéčhetu - it is about right, it is about that way; (pg 127)

waí → í; (pg 35, 45, 59, 79, 80, 129)

waíŋmnaŋke → íŋyaŋkA; (pg 62)

wak'ú → k'ú; (pg 80)

wakáǧapi - making things; (pg 65)

wakáǧe → káǧA; (pg 129)

wakáǧiŋ → káǧA; (pg 42)

wakáksaksa → kaksáksa; (pg 41, 42)

wakásto → kastó; (pg 13)

wakáyežu → kayéžu; (pg 80)

wakhí → khí; (pg 13)

wakhúl - hunting; (pg 23, 24)

wakȟókipȟA - to fear things; (pg 43)

wakpá - river; (pg 62)

wakpáhi → kpahí; (pg 54)

wakpála - creek; (pg 28)

wakpátakiya - toward the river; (pg 131)

wakšíča - bowl, plate; (pg 127)

wakšú 1 - to bead; (pg 39, 62, 63, 66, 67, 68, 85, 129)

Glossary

wakšú 2 - I beaded it

wakšúpi - beading; (pg 62, 65)

walówaŋ → lowáŋ; (pg 62)

wamákȟaškaŋ - animal; (pg, 24, 64, 95, 102)

wamátukȟa → watúkȟa; (pg 99)

wamáyazaŋ → wayázaŋ; (pg 100)

waná - now; (pg 32)

wanáȟča - flower; (pg 88)

wanáp'iŋ - necklace, pendant breastplate, neck ornament; (pg 48)

waníčA - there is none, to have none (with body parts); (pg 102, 103, 104, 106)

wanítukȟa → watúkȟa; (pg 99)

waníyazaŋ → wayázaŋ; (pg 100)

waníyetu - winter; year; (pg 32, 111, 117)

wanúŋwe → nuŋwÁŋ; (pg 62)

waŋ - a certain one

waŋbláke → waŋyáŋkA; (pg 2, 3, 13, 14, 24, 57)

waŋblí - eagle; (pg 29)

Waŋblí Paháh - Eagle Butte, SD; (pg 84)

wáŋčag - at once, immediately; (pg 127)

waŋčhíyaŋg → waŋyáŋkA; (pg 135)

waŋčhíyaŋke → waŋyáŋkA; (pg 35)

waŋglág → waŋglákA; (pg 98)

waŋglákA - to see one's own; (pg 13, 98)

waŋhíŋkpe - arrow; (pg 94)

waŋíč'iglakA - to see oneself; (pg 108)

waŋkátuya - to be high; (pg 110)

waŋláka → waŋyáŋkA; (pg 2)

waŋmáyalaka → waŋyáŋkA; (pg 35)

waŋmáyaŋg → waŋyáŋkA; (pg 4)

waŋmáyaŋkapi → waŋyáŋkA; (pg 26)

waŋmáyaŋke → waŋyáŋkA; (pg 14, 22, 24, 26, 35)

waŋná - now; (pg 32, 80, 85, 98, 127)

waŋníyaŋka → waŋyáŋkA; (pg 24)

waŋúŋyaŋkapi → waŋyáŋkA; (pg 111)

waŋúŋyaŋke → waŋyáŋkA; (pg 110)

waŋwíčhalaka → waŋyáŋkA; (pg 111)

waŋwíčhayaŋke → waŋyáŋkA; (pg 130)

waŋyáŋg → waŋyáŋkA; (pg 85)

waŋyáŋg yaŋkÁ - to sit watching smth/sb; (pg 85)

waŋyáŋkA - to see smth/sb; (pg 2, 24, 111)

waŋží 1 - one; (pg 122)

waŋží 2 - a, any; (pg 122)

waŋžígži - certain ones, one each; (pg 101)

waŋžígžila - only one each; (pg 113)

waŋžíni - no, none; (pg 13, 33, 133, 135)

waȟpé 1 - leaves; (pg 117)

waȟpé 2 - tea; (pg 127, 128, 129, 130, 132, 137)

waȟpé wókheya - arbor; (pg 59, 94)

waphégnake - hair ornament; (pg 53)

waphóštaŋ - hat; (pg 47)

waptáye - weeds; (pg 117)

waš'ákA - to be strong; (pg 108)

waškáŋ → škáŋ; (pg 42)

waskúyeča - candy, sweets; (pg 117)

wašté - to be good; (pg 70)

waštémna - to smell good; (pg 113)

waštéšte → wašté; (pg 80)

watȟáŋ - bait (as used in fishing or trapping); (pg 18)

wáte → yútA; (pg 56)

waȟtélašni - to dislike smth/sb; (pg 128)

wátiŋ → yútA; (pg 56)

watóhaŋlšna - sometimes; (pg 62)

watȟóka - vegetation, plants; (pg 117, 120)

watȟókeča - berries, fruits, wild fruits; (pg 89, 91)

watúkȟa - to be tired; (pg 96, 99,122)

waú → ú; (pg 135)

wa- - "I" personal affix for some verbs; (pg 133)

waúŋkšupi → wakšú; (pg 68)

waúŋyAŋ - to make an offering using smth; (pg 40)

waúŋyawa → wayáwa; (pg 111)

waúŋyutiŋ → wótA; (pg 85)

wawáči → wačhí; (pg 64)

wawákšu → wakšú; (pg 129)

wawóslata wanáp'iŋ - hair-pipe breastplate (with bones placed vertically, worn by women); (pg 53)

wayáčhi → wačhí; (pg 60, 62, 64, 68)

wayákšupi → **wakšú**; (pg 62)

wayášla - to graze (as cattle do); (pg 114)

wayáta → **wótA**; (pg 99)

wayátkAŋ - to drink things, compare with **yatkÁŋ**; (pg 32)

wayázaŋ - to be sick; (pg 100)

wayúȟičA - to wake people up; (pg 38)

wazí - pine; (pg 94)

wazíčhaŋ - pine tree; (pg 89)

wazílyA - to burn herbs ritually, to smudge; (pg 94)

wazíyapȟaȟli - icicle; (pg 93)

wéč'uŋ → **kič'úŋ**; (pg 59)

weló - marks an assertion spoken by a man; (pg 130)

wétu - spring (season); (pg 117)

wíčazo - pen; (pg 6, 49, 135)

wičháblužaža → **yužáža**; (pg 121)

wičhák'u → **k'ú**; (pg 101)

wičhášitȟokšu - bus; (pg 137)

wičháyuha → **yuhá**; (pg 13)

wičháyužaža → **yužáža**; (pg 121)

wičhíŋčala - girl; (pg 127)

wičhítenaškaŋškaŋ - movie, television; (pg 85)

wičhítenaškaŋškaŋ othí - movie theater; (pg 73)

wičhúŋkhuwapi → **khuwá**; (pg 24)

wičhúŋyužaža → **yužáža**; (pg 122)

wíglasto - hair brush; comb; (pg 100)

wígli - oil; (pg 80)

wígli oínažiŋ - gas station; (pg 74, 80, 84)

wígni - to search for things/food/provisions; (pg 120)

wihíŋpaspa - tent pegs; (pg 18, 20)

wíhupa - a handle; (pg 94)

wíkȟaŋ - rope; (pg 18, 19)

wíkičhiyuŋǧapi - to ask each other questions;→**wíyuŋǧA**; (pg 62)

wíŋyaŋ - woman; (pg 29)

wíŋyela - female; (pg 113)

wípatȟA - to do porcupine quillwork; (pg 119)

wíphi - to be filled or satisfied with food, to be full; (pg 70)

wítka - egg; (pg 124)

wiwáŋyaŋg wačhípi - Sundance; (pg 94)

wíyaka - feather; (pg 32)

wíyuŋǧA - to ask sb questions; (pg 62)

wo/we - marks command spoken by a male; (pg 100)

wóglakA - to speak, tell one's own things; (pg 111)

wóihaŋble - dream, vision; (pg 32, 42, 43)

woíle - to make smth (fire) blaze by blowing with the mouth; (pg 41)

wók'u - to feed sb/smth; (pg 5)

wókheya - shelter, arbor, lodge; (pg 94)

wókiyakA - to talk to sb, tell sb things; (pg 95)

wókȟokiphe - to be dangerous, fearful, scary; (pg 25)

wókȟoyake - costume; (pg 52)

wómak'u → **wók'u**; (pg 6)

wótA - to eat; (pg 32, 85, 99, 117)

wótiŋ → **wótA**; (pg 32)

wóuŋglakapi → **wóglakA**; (pg 111)

wóuŋspe - lesson; (pg 85)

wóuŋspe omnáye - computer; (pg 49, 85)

wówak'u → **wók'u**; (pg 13)

wówapi - book; letter; (pg 47, 111)

wówapi blawá → **wówapi yawá**; (pg 62)

wówapi othí - library; (pg 74)

wówapi yawá - to read books; (pg 65)

wówapi yawápi - reading books; (pg 65)

wówičhak'u → **wók'u**; (pg 121)

wówičhuŋk'u → **wók'u**; (pg 122)

wóyute - food; (pg 111, 113, 137)

wóžapi - traditional pudding; (pg 94, 127, 136)

wóžuha - bag; (pg 49)

yÁ - to go there; (pg 62, 85)

yačhíŋ → **čhíŋ**; (pg 134)

yaglúha → **gluhá**; (pg 49)

yaȟépA - to drink smth up; (pg 136, 127)

yaȟtákA - to bite sb/smth; (pg 25)

yaí → **í**; (pg 79)

yaíŋnaŋka → **íŋyaŋkA**; (pg 68)

yakáǧiŋ → **káǧA**; (pg 42)

yakú → **kú**; (pg 42)

yalówaŋ → **lowáŋ**; (pg 62)

Glossary

yámni - three; (pg 90)

yanúŋwaŋ → nuŋwÁŋ; (pg 62)

yaŋkÁ - to sit, be sitting; (pg 67, 80, 85, 111)

yápi → yÁ; (pg 74, 84)

yátiŋ → yútA; (pg 42)

yatkÁŋ - to drink smth; (pg 49, 136)

ya- - you; (pg 133)

yaúŋ → úŋ; (pg 43)

yawá - to read smth; (pg 62)

yažópi - playing on smth by blowing; (pg 39)

yé 1 → yÁ; (pg 77)

ye 2 - marks command; (pg 77)

yélakȟa - must have; (pg 25)

yeló - assertion spoken by a man; (pg 95)

yetȟó - familiar command spoken by a man, see nitȟó; (pg 135)

yíŋ → yÁ; (pg 32, 73)

yuğáŋ - to open smth; (pg 50, 130)

yuhá - to have or keep smth; to keep sb; (pg 13)

yuȟíčA - to wake sb up; (pg 36, 38)

yuȟláȟla - to make smth ring/rattle; (pg 51)

yuȟlátA - to scratch smth with fingernails or claws; (pg 25)

yuȟ'í - to have a rough or chapped surface; (pg 103, 104)

yuȟ'íȟ'i → yuȟ'í; (pg 103)

yuílepi - matches; (pg 41)

yukȟÁŋ - there is, it exists, a body part exists for one; (pg 102, 106, 120)

yuk'éȟk'eğA - to scratch smth repeatedly; (pg 126)

yúl → yútA; (pg 117)

yuŋkȟáŋ - and here, and then; (pg 14, 15, 24, 27, 43)

yuš'íŋš'iŋ - to tickle sb; (pg 108)

yuš'íŋyemaye → yuš'íŋyeyA; (pg 22)

yuš'íŋyeyA - to surprise or startle sb; (pg 6)

yušíčA - to spoil or damage smth; (pg 136)

yušlá - to pluck smth (as weeds); (pg 40, 43)

yušlášla → yušlá; (pg 40)

yustósto - to stroke or pet smth/sb; (pg 70)

yútA - to eat smth; (pg 28, 56, 117, 118, 127, 136)

yútiŋ → yútA; (pg 127)

yuwí - to wrap or bandage smth; (pg 25)

yužáža - to wash smth/sb; (pg 49, 119, 121)

yužúŋ - to pull smth up with the roots, to pluck, extract (as a tooth); (pg 119)

yužúžu - to unwrap smth, to pull smth apart; (pg 122)

záŋgzaŋka - to whine, whimper; (pg 121)

zaŋní - to be healthy; (pg 122)

žaŋžáŋla - to be transparent, translucent; (pg 122)

záptaŋ - five; (pg 122)

zí - to be yellow; (pg 122)

zibzípela - to be thin; (pg 89, 129)

zičá - squirrel; (pg 44)

ziŋtkála - bird; (pg 103, 114)

zizí → zí; (pg 122)

žiží - to be fair-haired, have tawny hair; (pg 122)

zizípela - to be thin, fine (as a blade, beads, cloth); (pg 122)

žožó - to whistle; (pg 122)

zuzéča - snake; (pg 114, 122)

Activity sheet for Wóuŋspe 4, Pg 53, Ex 22

20 Think about a man and a woman in your family who are dancers. Take out a piece of scrap paper and draw their regalia. Then, write a description, like the model. If you do not know any dancers, use your imagination.

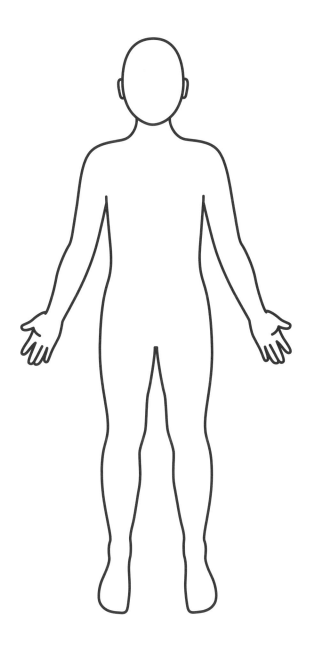
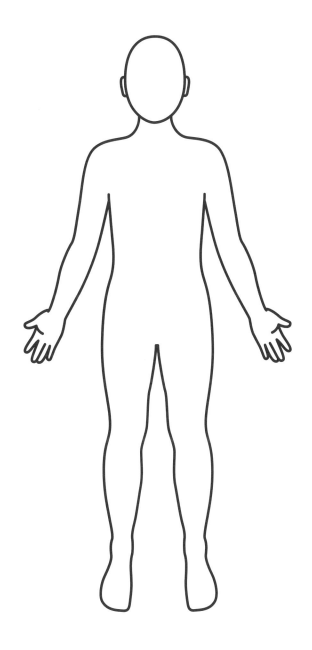

_____   _____

_____   _____

_____   _____

Appendix

Wówaši nitȟáwa:
očhéthi waŋží káǧa yo/ye

Lená luhá:

Lená yačhíŋ:

Wówaši nitȟáwa:
ȟtawóhaŋ yo/ye

Lená luhá:

Lená yačhíŋ:

Wówaši nitȟáwa:
thiyóbleča kiŋ pawóslal iyéya yo/ye

Lená luhá:

Lená yačhíŋ:

Wówaši nitȟáwa:
čhaŋáuŋpi/čhaŋókpaŋ etáŋ aú wo/we

Lená luhá:

Lená yačhíŋ:

Wówaši nitȟáwa:
wíčhokaŋ hiyáya wótapi lol'íȟ'aŋ yo/ye

Lená luhá:

Lená yačhíŋ:

Wówaši nitȟáwa:
hokȟúwa yo/ye

Lená luhá:

Lená yačhíŋ:

Wówaši nitȟáwa:
thiyóbleča kiŋ wíŋyeya égle yo/ye

Lená luhá:

Lená yačhíŋ:

Wówaši nitȟáwa:
čhethí yo/ye

Lená luhá:

Lená yačhíŋ:

Appendix

Activity cards for Wóuŋspe 3, pg 39, Ex 20

I want someone to teach me:

I want someone to teach me:

I want someone to teach me:

I want someone to teach me:

I want someone to teach me:

I want someone to teach me:

I want someone to teach me:

I want someone to teach me:

Appendix

Ȟtálehaŋ - Lisa

Haŋhépi - Bob

Híŋhaŋni - Summer

Wíčhokaŋ hiyáye k'uŋ héhaŋ - Mike

Okó k'uŋ héhaŋ - James

Aŋpétu núŋpa k'uŋ héhaŋ - Ťhašína

Blokétu k'uŋ héhaŋ - Matȟó

Wí k'uŋ héhaŋ - Kimi